CATERPILLAR

ERIC C. ORLEMANN

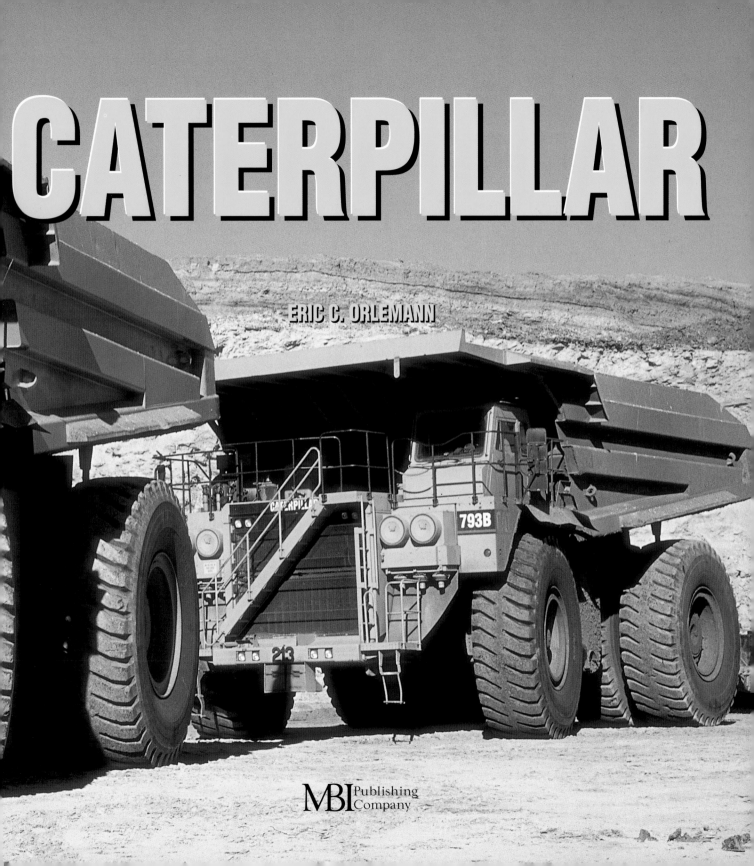

MBI Publishing Company

First published in 1998 by MBI Publishing Company, 729 Prospect Avenue, PO Box 1, Osceola, WI 54020-0001 USA

MBI Publishing Company books are also available at discounts in bulk quantity for industrial or sales-promotional use. For details write to Special Sales Manager at Motorbooks International Wholesalers & Distributors, 729 Prospect Avenue, PO Box 1, Osceola, WI 54020-0001 USA.

Library of Congress Cataloging-in-Publication Data

Orlemann, Eric C.
        Caterpillar/ Eric Orlemann.
                p. cm.-- (Enthusiast color series)
        Includes index.
        ISBN 0-7603-0529-3 (pbk. : alk. paper)
        1. Earthmoving machinery--History. 2. Caterpillar Inc. 3. Construction Equipment--United States--History. 4. Earthmoving machinery--Pictorial works 5. Construction equipment--United States--Pictorial works.
        I. Series.
TA725065   1998
    629.225--dc21   98-3913

Text by Eric Orlemann
Photos by Eric Orlemann, unless credited otherwise

On the front cover: The Caterpillar D10R dozer introduced in 1996 and powered by a V-12 Cat 3412E diesel engine, has majestically moved massive amounts of earth. It produces 570 fhp horsepower and has an average operating weight of 144,986 pounds. This is the first unit delivered into service, working at a coal mine in Powder River Basin, Wyoming. *Eric C. Orlemann*

On the frontispiece: The D9 series is a machine with serious "grunt," and it is one of the machines that has made Caterpillar a player in today's earthmoving market. This D9N (1JD) is powered by a Cat 3408 diesel engine rated at 370 fhp horsepower. It shows how to get the job done, as it pulls its ripping shank through solid rock. *Urs Peyer*

On the title page: A pair of colossal 240-ton capacity Caterpillar 793B haul trucks are pictured during a brief stop for the afternoon shift change at a coal mine located in the Powder River Basin mining area of Wyoming. *ECO*

On the back cover: A massive P&H 2800XPA electric mining shovel loads overburden into a huge Caterpillar 793B haul truck. It takes only four passes from the shovel's 43 cubic-yard bucket to fully load the 240-ton capacity hauler and send it on its way. *ECO*

Edited by Paul Johnson
Designed by Tom Heffron

Printed in Hong Kong through World Print, Ltd.

CONTENTS

ACKNOWLEDGMENTS

In the course of my career, I have come to know many people associated with Caterpillar. Over the years, they have provided a wealth of information and materials, and this project was no different. Some went to extreme lengths, above and beyond the call of duty, to meet with me, concerning various research needs for this book. I would like to thank the following individuals, both from Caterpillar, Inc. and from its various dealers, for helping me make this endeavor a reality. They are Pete J. Holman, John Ingle, Jeff Hawkinson, Joycelyn A. Luster, Bob Muntz, Mark. W. Sprouls, Jeff C. Drake, Shane L. Ham, Ted Rogers, Elaine Barnett, Mary Alice Kuntz, Josy Applegate, Mark Miller, and Tom Novak.

I would also like to thank the following people who are not associated with Caterpillar, Inc. for their time and effort in the various location photography set-ups. They are Christine L. Taylor, Bob Heimann, David A. Thomas, and Bill Suter.

Keith Haddock, Don Frantz, Ron Ketron, and Tom Peirce of the Historical Construction Equipment Association (H.C.E.A.), truly deserve a special thanks for research assistance and equipment procurement.

Finally, I would like to express my deepest appreciation to the following individuals for supplying photographic images, in addition to my own work, that helped to tell the story of Caterpillar. My thanks goes out to, Urs Peyer, and especially Randy Leffingwell, for coming to my rescue concerning Best and Holt. A job well done, I must say.

–Eric C. Orlemann

INTRODUCTION

Caterpillar. The name alone conjures up a vision of majestic large, yellow, tracked machines pushing massive amounts of earth, literally moving mountains, and changing the world in which we live. Only a few companies in the world, when their names are spoken, are so closely identified with the products they manufacture. When one thinks of Ford, we picture an automobile; John Deere, a farm tractor; Mack, a heavy duty truck; and Caterpillar, a bulldozer. Name recognition like this is one of the most sought after, and elusive, attributes in the manufacturing sector. But as with Caterpillar, all you have to do is hear the word, and look at the tracks moving on one of its crawler dozers, and the association is made instantly. It is the perfect name.

Caterpillar, Inc. is the largest and most profitable producer of heavy-duty earthmoving equipment in the world today. The company's global sales and marketing strategy is always exploring new market niches. Caterpillar employs over 16,500 people directly, who work in dozens of factories worldwide. The heart of the company's manufacturing base is the plants located in the cities of East Peoria, Decatur, Aurora, and Joliet, Illinois, with Peoria serving as the worldwide corporate headquarters. Peoria has often been referred to as the "earthmoving capitol of the world."

The product lines that are included in this book represent the "classic" earthmoving and agricultural equipment built by Caterpillar over the years. These include dozers, motor graders, scrapers, wheel loaders, haulers, excavators, and some agricultural machines. These categories represent the established and well-known lines offered by the company. It does not mean that other Caterpillar products hold less value, but that the enthusiasm and popular interest for large dozers and haulers are greater than, let's say, asphalt pavers.

Caterpillar equipment depicted in this book represents some of the key historical machines, plus many of the largest built or offered in a given product line. Due to space limitations, not every model can be illustrated with an image. Instead, greater attention has been paid to the larger equipment built by the company, since this is where the greatest interest lies.

Throughout the early chapters of the book, some of the models' names are listed with a number and letter combination called the "Product Identification Number Prefix." This prefix code is an identifying feature of the serial number that determines the model. In many instances, the nomenclature for a given machine is the same, but the prefix number is different. This can mean various things, such as a different engine, gearbox, power curve, build location, etc. This number has been included with many of the earlier Caterpillar offerings, especially the gas-powered crawlers, in the hopes that some of the confusion between these various models can be lessened.

This project is meant to celebrate some of Caterpillar's greatest equipment offerings and designs, and is not intended to be a "corporate history" of the company's business dealings. For a more in-depth look at the early beginnings of the Caterpillar history, I highly recommend seeking out Randy Leffingwell's book *Caterpillar*, also published by MBI Publishing.

Horsepower Ratings

My primary goal in writing this book is to make the information as understandable as possible. To accomplish that end, I compiled this brief glossary that explains horsepower references used throughout the book. In measuring a machine's power output, there are different types of horsepower ratings assigned for a specific purposes. In the heavy equipment and agricultural industry, the following types of ratings are the most widely used in North America:

Gross horsepower: Gross horsepower is the output of the engine or motor as installed in the machine *without* the major accessories connected.

Flywheel horsepower (fhp): Flywheel horsepower, sometimes referred to as net horsepower, is the actual horsepower output *with* all accessories connected, including the fan, air compressor, generator, and hydraulic pump. This rating is the one most used when comparing one model to another.

Drawbar horsepower: Drawbar horsepower is the machine's flywheel horsepower minus friction and slippage losses in the drive mechanism and the tracks or tires.

PTO horsepower: This power rating is measured at the "Power Take-Off" connection from the engine and/or transmission, often found at the rear of the tractor. PTO horsepower is more often used in reference with agricultural machinery.

CHAPTER 1

Holt plus Best equals Caterpillar Tractor Company

Caterpillar, as a corporate entity, can trace its roots back directly to the lush and fertile farm valleys of California in the late-1880s. It was during this time period that the horse and mule teams were about to start giving way to steam-powered machines. The competition for sales in this new market, between two individuals in particular, would set the stage for the birth of a new company whose name would become synonymous with the terms "crawler-tractor" and "bulldozer." These men were Daniel Best and Benjamin Holt.

When he was in his early 20s, Daniel Best left his home in Iowa to go west and seek his fortune. Like many before him, the lure of various and unique business opportunities, and of course gold, enticed many men, including Daniel Best, to leave

This beautifully restored Best Steamer is a 1904 vintage traction engine, rated at 110 horsepower from its steam-powered two-cylinder engine. The tank in the front holds 940 gallons of water for the boiler. Overall length of the Steamer is 28 feet. Randy Leffingwell

The Holt Model 40 tractor, S.N. 1003 was the first gas-powered unit sold by Holt in 1908. The first working prototype of the Holt gas tractor dated back to December 1906. Caterpillar, Inc.

their homes and move to Oregon, Washington, and California.

After arriving in Steptoville (currently Walla Walla), Washington, Best sought out work at a lumber mill, since this is what he knew best because he had worked in the family's sawmill while in his teens. After a try at his own mill, Best set out for Portland, Oregon, where he found himself working at another lumber mill. Again, not satisfied with his occupation, Best and a partner invested in a gold mine in southern Washington. Here he achieved some success until he lost his gold, and almost his life, when his raft capsized in some rough river waters.

Best floated between various mining and lumbering jobs between 1862 and 1869, with some prov-

ing profitable and others not. He would eventually wind up in Marysville, California, where he started to work with his brother, Henry, on his ranch in 1869.

After the ranch's grain harvest, Best's brother, and all of the other surrounding farms, transported their grain into town to be cleaned. This was necessary before the grain could be sold. Best began to think that there must be a quicker, easier, more cost-effective way. He thought maybe the key was not to take the grain into town to be cleaned, but to bring the cleaner to the farm or, to be more exact, into the field.

After working through the winter with his brothers, Best was ready to start testing his transportable cleaner concept machines in that year's grain harvest. So successful was the cleaner's performance that Best applied for, and received, a patent on his design in April 1871.

After some brief career diversions, Best was back in the fields designing ever-larger harvesters for the farmers of California. To meet the farmers' needs, the harvesters were becoming quite large; so large, in fact, that the horse teams could barely pull them through the fields. What was needed was more horsepower, and not of the animal kind.

In 1888, Best witnessed a demonstration of a steam traction engine designed by a blacksmith named Marquis De Lafayette Remington. Best was

so impressed with what was called the "Rough and Ready," he purchased the rights to build the traction engine with an agreement that he would not sell it in Remington's home state of Oregon. The Best traction engine and combined harvester made an impressive team, and in late 1889 Best sold his first steam traction engine.

The road fate had laid out for Benjamin Holt to take in his business endeavors was not as eclectic as that of Best's. Holt got his career start by joining his father's business in Concord, New Hampshire, which was in lumber, specializing in hardwoods for wagon building. In 1869, Holt's brother Charles

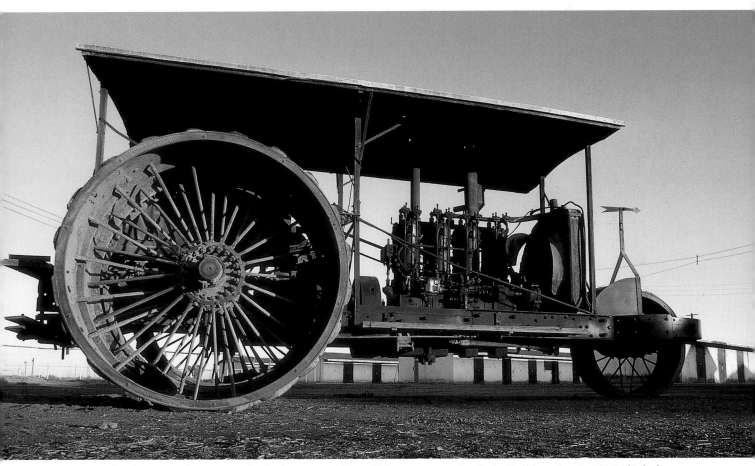

First introduced in 1910, the Best Round Wheel was powered by a 60-horsepower gas six-cylinder Buffalo engine. By 1913, this had been replaced by a more powerful Best-designed 75-horsepower four-cylinder unit. This 1910 Best Round Wheel tractor was the 51st built, and is currently powered by the 75-horsepower engine. It was initially equipped with the 60-horsepower engine, but later the owner had it removed and replaced with the 75-horsepower unit. Randy Leffingwell

The Best 75 Tracklayer was first released in 1912 and produced a claimed 75 horsepower from its gas engine. The 75 weighed in at 28,000 pounds and was 23-feet, 9-inches in length. The 1917 vintage model shown here is one of but a few Tracklayers still in existence today. Randy Leffingwell

started up a new company called C. H. Holt & Company in San Francisco, specializing in the sale of hardwoods, which were purchased from his father's company and sold to various wagon and boat manufacturers in the area. Unfortunately, the climate of the area was not well suited for the seasoning of the lumber, so a new home for the company was found farther inland in Stockton. In 1883, the Holt brothers established the Stockton Wheel Company, with Benjamin brought over from the family's business in Concord to head it up.

In 1886, the company released "The Holt Bros. Improved Link Belt Combined Harvester," which utilized linked chains and sprockets instead of conventional belt-driven pulleys. This helped eliminate problems with slipping belts under load. Another Holt invention in 1890 was the "side-hill" harvester, which helped farmers better utilize all of their available acreage. At the same time as the side-hill machines were developed, Holt began building a steam traction engine that he invented, nicknamed "Old Betsy." It featured something the other manufacturers did not offer—steering clutches. In 1892, the Holt brothers' company name was changed from the Stockton Wheel Company to The Holt Manufacturing Company, which reflected the ever-expanding product developments offered by the firm. All of this was overseen by Benjamin Holt, who was now the company's president.

The steam traction engines, built by both Best and Holt, worked well in the fields when on dry and stable ground. But in peat, or other soft soils, these tremendously heavy machines would get mired down in the fields. A temporary solution to this problem was the fitting of extremely wide rim extensions, which provided better flotation. Both Best and Holt used these on their tractors, but the tractors still were not perfect. Something else was needed. And that something was tracks.

On November 24, 1904, Holt started testing a modified version of his No. 77 wheel-type steamer minus the rear wheels. In place of the wheels was a set of tracks made from malleable link belts with wooden blocks attached to act as treads. A photographer by the name of Charles Clements was taking pictures of the tractor during its testing, and said that the movement of the tracks reminded him of an undulating caterpillar. Once Holt heard the remark made by Clements, he knew he had found a name for his newest creation. Thus, the name Caterpillar was born.

Additional prototypes (six in all) of Holt's track-type tractors were built and tested throughout 1905 and 1906. By the end of 1906, the seventh Holt Brothers Paddle Wheel Improved Traction Engine No. 111 was built and sold to a paying customer, making this the first true production model.

Another technological breakthrough at the time was the gasoline engine. Holt was impressed—so impressed that he and one of his nephews, Pliny Holt, established another company, the Aurora Engine Company, in Stockton, California, which was integrated into Holt Manufacturing in 1913. Aurora continued development of the gas engine concept in October 1906, and two months later the original prototype was first tested. In early 1908, the second unit was built. Later that year, the third gas tractor, the Holt Model 40, was shipped to a

customer making it the first gas Caterpillar tractor sold. By 1910, Holt's gas-powered tractors had firmly established themselves in the marketplace.

The bitter rivalry between these two tractor competitors came to a head and spilled over into the courtroom in 1905, when Best filed a lawsuit against Holt for patent infringement. The case went back and forth in the courts during 1906 and 1907, producing various verdicts and many appeals. But before a final ruling came down, both Best and Holt agreed to settle the dispute and began talking about the feasibility of combining their companies. By this time, Daniel Best was 70 years old and thought that it might be a good time in his life to sell his interest in Best Manufacturing to Holt. On October 8, 1908, the business was sold to Benjamin and Charles Holt, but not before Daniel Best made sure that his son, Clarence Leo Best, would be the new president of The Holt Manufacturing Company's San Leandro, California, facilities, though the Holts would still maintain ultimate control of the firm.

Expansion was on the minds of the Holts and a new company location was found that fit their needs nicely. The Colean Manufacturing Company of East Peoria, Illinois, was in the middle of bankruptcy proceedings. Colean's factory was relatively new and suited Holt's needs, since the company had once built threshers and steamers. On October 25, 1909, the deal was finalized that would make Peoria the firm's new headquarters. When the company finally incorporated in Illinois the following January, it would carry the new name of The Holt Caterpillar Company. In 1910, the "Caterpillar" term was officially registered as a company trademark.

C.L. Best was not happy with the way things were working out for him at Holt, and he finally decided to leave the company in 1910. C.L. Best relocated to Elmhurst, California, and established a new company of his own called C.L. Best Gas Traction Company. Initially, Best built 60-horsepower, and then 75-horsepower, wheel-type gas-powered tractors, but by 1912 he had introduced his first tracked model—the C.L.B. 75HP "Tracklayer." In fact, Best's 75 Tracklayer incorporated many advanced features not found in the Holt machines.

Best made a patent application on some of the Tracklayer features in 1913, which was granted to him on August 8, 1916. These tractors proved so popular that Best was able to repurchase his father's larger former plant at San Leandro in mid-1916, which increased his manufacturing output considerably.

Between 1910 and 1925, both The Holt Caterpillar Company and the C.L. Best Gas Traction Company released many noteworthy gas-powered tracked machines. Some of the more popular tractors introduced by Holt included the Holt Model 40 in 1908; the Model 45 in 1910; the Model 60 in 1911; the Model 30 "Baby Holt" in 1912; the Model 75 and

Model 18 in 1914; the Model 120 in 1915; the Models T-11/T-29 (Holt 5 Ton) and Holt 10 Ton in 1918; and the T-35 (Holt 2 Ton) in 1921. C.L. Best machines that were well received by the public were the Best C.L.B. 75 in 1912; the 40 in 1914; the 25 in 1918; and the legendary C.L. Best 60 and 30 models introduced in 1919 and 1921, respectively.

The war years between 1914 and 1918 greatly affected production and the future of both companies. Holt's business was at full capacity, but mainly due to large military contracts. This was fine while the war was going on, but when it ended, Holt was left with piles of canceled government contracts, and tractors that were far better suited for pulling

First introduced in 1914, the Holt Model 75 "Caterpillar" was Holt's answer to C.L. Best's 75 Tracklayer. The Model 75 tractor was a real workhorse with its 75-horsepower gas engine. This 1917 version is pictured pulling a "Holt Land Leveler" grader. Randy Leffingwell

In 1919, C.L. Best built one of the greatest gas-powered tractors—the Best 60. Even though the Best four-cylinder engine was supposed to develop 60 horsepower, it actually never bettered 56.3 horsepower when initially tested by the University of Nebraska. The 17,500-pound crawler became a Caterpillar Model Sixty in 1925, and continued in production until 1931. Randy Leffingwell

artillery than plowing fields. Best, on the other hand, had been given permission to continue building his farm tractors, which gave him a big advantage over Holt when the war ended.

After World War I, the U.S. economy began to slip into an economic recession. With surplus military tractors flooding the market at practically giveaway prices, it was increasingly hard to sell new machines. The shrinking economy was putting the squeeze on both tractor manufacturers, weakening both firms financially. With the future of both companies at stake, they discussed combining forces to weather the hard times. On April 15, 1925, legal papers were officially filed that would merge, or more accurately consolidate, both the Holt Caterpillar Company and C. L. Best Gas Traction Company into a new single corporate entity, to be named the Caterpillar Tractor Company.

CHAPTER 2

The Crawler Tractors, Dozers, and Loaders

After the merger of the Holt Caterpillar Company and C. L. Best Gas Traction Company, the first thing the Caterpillar Tractor Company had to do was to decide which models were going to stay, and which were to go. The larger Best 30 and 60 models were retained in the product line and would become the Caterpillar Model Thirty and the Model Sixty. Initially the Holt 2-Ton, 5-Ton, and 10-Ton tractors became Caterpillar machines, but within months, the 5-Ton and 10-Ton tractors were discontinued. These models were considered somewhat outdated compared to the Best designs and were too expensive to manufacture. By late 1925, Caterpillar was listing sales prices for three tractors: the Thirty, the Sixty, and the 2-Ton.

The Diesel Seventy-Five was the largest crawler in the product line when it was first introduced in 1933. It stayed in production until it was replaced by the RD-8 in late 1935. Pictured working in California in late 1934 is a 98-horsepower Diesel Seventy-Five equipped with an R.G. LeTourneau Angledozer blade attachment. ECO collection

In 1928, Caterpillar introduced the Model Ten (PT) that was powered by an 18.72-horsepower gas engine. It was replaced in 1932 by the 21.6-horsepower Cat Model Fifteen (7C). In the background is a 77-horsepower gas-powered Caterpillar Model Sixty, first introduced as the C.L. Best 60 in 1919. Production ended on the Sixty in 1931. Both tractors shown here are 1929 vintage models. Randy Leffingwell

Caterpillar Gas-Engined Tractors

As the models before them, all of Caterpillar's crawler-tractors utilized gasoline-fueled engines in the early years of the company, with numerous models and variations introduced over the next few years. So many in fact, it would be impossible to go into any great detail on all of them in this text and verse. What is important though, is the evolution of the different model types, and how they were incorporated into the Caterpillar product line.

The Caterpillar Model Ten (PT) was the smallest of the gas tractors. It was produced from 1928 to 1932, and sold rather well when compared to other Cat offerings, but was troubled with annoying design shortcomings that plagued the tractor over its entire production run.

Introduced in 1929, the Caterpillar Model Fifteen (PV) was, for all intents and purposes, just a larger Model Ten. It also suffered many of the same shortcomings as its smaller sibling. Production on the Fifteen ended in 1932.

The replacement for the Model Ten, introduced in 1932, was the Caterpillar Model Fifteen (7C). The 7C Model Fifteen was not the same as the PV Model Fifteen from 1929, and was actually smaller than that unit. It was only in production until 1933.

This 1936 vintage Caterpillar RD-4 (which also happens to be the first year of release for this series) is equipped with an R.G. LeTourneau WC4 Angledozer blade attachment. The tractor developed 41.17 horsepower from its diesel engine. The RD-4 became the Cat D4 in late 1937. Randy Leffingwell

Many of the design flaws originally found in the PV Model Fifteen series of machines were addressed in 1932 with the release of its replacement, the Caterpillar Model Twenty (8C). Production ended on this tractor in 1934.

The Caterpillar Model Twenty (L and PL) was the first totally new design to be released by the company, and was not related to the 8C Model Twenty. The "L" serial number prefix ID code stood for Model Twentys built at the San Leandro, California, plant starting in 1927, while the "PL" prefix represented tractors assembled at the Peoria, Illinois, factory, which started production on this model in 1928. Both series of crawlers ended their production runs in 1931.

Caterpillar's most popular small gas crawler-tractor, at least as far as the number of units sold is concerned, was the Model Twenty-Two (2F and 1J). This crawler was in production from 1934 to 1939, with about 15,156 total machines built. Its smart design and overall reliability made it a standout performer.

Related to the Model Twenty-Two was the Caterpillar Model R-2 (5E), built from 1934 to 1937. The Model R-2 was very similar mechanically to a wide-gauge Model Twenty-Two. Since the R-2 was government specified, most were destined for military service.

In late 1931, a redesignated version of the PL Model Twenty was introduced, called the Caterpillar Twenty-Five (3C). Both tractors were mechanically

The D7 was the new designation assigned to the RD-7 in late 1937. Power ratings remained at 82 horsepower for both models until the 93-horsepower Cat D7 (7M) was introduced in 1940. This D7 (9G) is a 1939 vintage model. Randy Leffingwell

the same, only some of the sheet metal had changed on the new unit. Production on the Model Twenty-Five ceased in 1933.

The replacement for the Model Twenty-Five was the Caterpillar Model Twenty-Eight (4F), which entered service in 1933. The Model Twenty-Eight version was the last of the tractors to be based on the old Model Twenty series (L and PL). Production lasted only until 1935.

A close cousin, design-wise, to the Model Twenty-Eight was the Caterpillar Model R-3 (5E2), which was available only from 1934 to 1935. The Model R-3 was a special government-ordered tractor, with only about 60 units listed as built.

The Caterpillar Model Thirty (S and PS) originally started out as the C. L. Best 30 from 1921, and was one of the first "Caterpillar" tractors. The "S"

prefix versions of the Model Thirty were built in San Leandro from 1921 to 1930, and the "PS" tractors were assembled in Peoria from 1926 to 1932. The Model Thirty was a very successful crawler, both for Caterpillar and for Best.

Introduced in 1935, the Caterpillar Model Thirty (6G) was in fact a completely redesigned PS Model Thirty, which had been out of production for three years. During the production run of the 6G Model Thirty, the designation of the unit was changed to the Model R-4. The prefix code was unchanged. Many of these tractors would find their homes in various government agencies because of World War II supply needs. Production ended in 1944.

In 1932, the Caterpillar Model Thirty-Five (5C) took the place of the old PS Model Thirty. The new

Caterpillar tractors were first offered with Cat-designed hydraulic blade controls in 1947 as an alternative to cable-controlled units. This D7 is shown with the early design Cat No. 7S Bulldozer and No. 46 Hydraulic Control. This added an extra 5,850 pounds to the D7's 24,630-pound tractor weight. Urs Peyer

tractor utilized most of the old Model Thirty's frame and engine, but the sheet metal was all new. Production ceased in 1934.

The Caterpillar Model Forty (5G) from 1934 replaced the Model Thirty-Five in the product line. Sales were sluggish on the Model Forty, with most new buyers preferring the Cat Diesel Forty instead of the gas-powered version, which ended production in 1936.

Related in size to the Model Thirty-Five and Model Forty tractors, was the Caterpillar Model R-5 (5E3, 4H, and 3R), which was built from 1934 to 1936 for all three of its versions. A portion of the 4H prefix code units and the 3R models were considered the gasoline alternatives to the diesel-powered RD-6 tractors in the Cat product line.

One of the larger gas tractors offered by Caterpillar in the 1930s was the Model Fifty (5A), which was produced from 1931 to 1937. Only a small quantity of Model Fifty gas units were built, mainly because of the switchover of customer loyalty to the diesel-engined models that were becoming more popular.

By far the most famous of the early gas tractors built by Caterpillar was the Model Sixty (A and PA), which was another of the original Cat machines first built by Best. The "A" prefix code versions were first produced as the C. L. Best 60 in 1919, at the San Leandro plant. The "PA" Caterpillar versions were built in Peoria starting in 1925. Both series runs ended in 1931. In its early years, this tractor was the chief rival to the Holt 10-Ton crawler.

Introduced in 1932, the Caterpillar Model Sixty-Five (2D) was a modified version of the popular Model Sixty, with redesigned sheet metal. Sales of the Sixty-Five were slow because of the switchover to diesel-powered models, and because many of the company's customers thought the Sixty-Five's appearance was controversial. Production ended in 1933.

The Caterpillar Model Seventy (8D) was introduced in 1933 as the replacement for the Model Sixty-Five. Sheet metal designs were changed back to that of the Model Sixty because of customer complaints about the Model Sixty-Five's appearance. Production finally ended in 1937. Again, interest in the diesel-engined tractors killed off the gas Model Seventy.

The D8H was an immensely popular dozer for Caterpillar when it replaced the D8G in 1958. This 1958 D8H (36A) dozer is equipped with the cable-controlled Cat No. 8A Angling-type Bulldozer. The D8H was powered by a six-cylinder, turbocharged Cat Model D342 diesel engine rated at 235 fhp. Either a six-speed Direct Drive, a three-speed Torque Converter Drive, or a three-speed Power Shift transmission could be specified. Average tractor weight was 47,220 pounds, plus an additional 8,360 pounds for the blade and controls. Randy Leffingwell

This Cat D9E (34A) needs only a can of ether and a set of jumper cables to put it back to work after its long intervals of idleness between jobs. The D9E replaced the 320-fhp D9D in mid-1959, and was powered by a six-cylinder, turbocharged Cat diesel engine rated at 335 fhp. Transmission choices were Power Shift (pictured), Direct Drive, or Torque Converter Drive. This unit is also equipped with a cable-controlled Cat No. 9S Bulldozer blade. Approximate weight of the D9E is 61,272 pounds, plus an additional 10,910 pounds for the blade and controls, totaling 72,182 pounds. ECO

The D9G (66A) replaced the D9E in 1961. Power was supplied by the six-cylinder, turbocharged, aftercooled Cat D353 diesel engine that produced 385 fhp at 1,330 rpm. The only transmission choice was a three-speed planetary-type Power Shift unit. The D9G shown is equipped with a Cat 9C Cushion Bulldozer blade with the single cylinder 193 Hydraulic Control, and the No. 9B Single Shank Beam, Parallelogram-type Ripper. This D9G is ideally suited as a push-tractor for high-production scraper loading. Overall working weight of this unit is 90,100 pounds. ECO

The Caterpillar D9H (90V) replaced the G series in mid-1974. The Cat D353 diesel engine pumped out more horsepower, now rated at 410 fhp. This D9H is equipped with a full-U, 9U Bulldozer blade and double-cylinder 9C Hydraulic Control. Average overall working weight, including ROPS (Roll Over Protective Structure) cab and multishank ripper, is 109,690 pounds. Urs Peyer

Starting in 1925, all of Caterpillar's gas tractors were painted a medium-gray color, with most trimmed in red. This was somewhat standard until December 1931 when the first plant memo announced that from then on, all new tractors leaving the factory were to be painted in bright "Hi-Way Yellow" with black trim.

And so was born the Caterpillar Yellow paint scheme.

Diesel-Engined Tractors

Caterpillar had taken a keen interest in the advantages of the diesel engine as a possible power source for its tractors. The diesel engine was already establishing itself in Europe and was beginning to make its presence known in the United States. The company thought that diesel power was the future for earth-moving crawlers and started engineering and research funding in 1926 for the development of its own diesel engine.

By mid-1931, Caterpillar had its first prototype diesel-engined tractor ready for testing—the Model Diesel Sixty (1C). Tests confirmed that the diesel-powered tractor cut fuel costs in half when compared to a gas-engined unit. The Diesel Sixty also exhibited power characteristics that were superior to those of a gas engine. The diesel was a real lugging machine, with a tremendous torque curve. But despite all of the good news, two things slowed the sales of these tractors—their high price and poor-quality diesel fuels. Eventually the prices came down, and thanks to Caterpillar's research and testing, more uniform diesel fuels, better suited to the hard working life of a crawler-tractor, were now being formulated by the large oil producers.

The early Caterpillar Model Diesel Sixty was upgraded into the Model Diesel Sixty-Five in 1932. Additional diesel tractor introductions included the Caterpillar Model Diesel Thirty-Five (6E), from 1933 to 1934; the Diesel Forty (3G), from 1934 to late 1935; the Diesel Fifty (1E), from 1933 to late 1935; the Diesel Seventy (3E), for 1933 only; and the Diesel Seventy-Five (2E), from 1933 to late 1935.

By the mid-1930s, Caterpillar diesel tractor developments were introduced, one right after another. Starting in late 1935, the Model Diesel Forty was changed into the Model RD-6 (2H); the Diesel Fifty became the Model RD-7 (9G); and the Diesel Seventy-Five turned into the Model RD-8 (1H). These new designations were officially introduced in the 1936 product line. Also released in 1936 was the smaller Model RD-4 (4G) series.

In late 1937, the tractor product line received all new model designations: the RD-4 changed into the D4; the RD-6 became the D6; the RD-7 changed

For push-loading scrapers through the most difficult working conditions, Caterpillar offered two tractors connected together in late 1964, called the Quad-Track D9G. In 1968, the designation was officially changed to the DD9G (90J front/91J rear). Utilizing the same engine type found in the D9G, the DD9G had the combined power of two drivetrains, producing a total output of 770 fhp. The DD9G was replaced in 1974 by the DD9H (97V front/98V rear), which produced a whopping 820 fhp. The DD9G weighed in at 176,900 pounds and the DD9H tipped the scales at 178,800 pounds. This rare DD9G is shown working in late 1993 in northern Kentucky, and is one of the few quads still operating in the world today. ECO

Big reclamation jobs call for a big bulldozer. Caterpillar's answer was the side-by-side dozer, called the SxS D9G. The SxS D9G (29N left side/30N right) factory production started in 1969 and ended in 1974 when the model was replaced by the more powerful SxS D9H (99V left/12U right). Drivetrains were the same as the ones found in the regular single tractors and quad units. Power output for the SxS D9G was 770 fhp and the H model was rated at 820 fhp. The tractors were connected together in three places: in the rear by a tie-bar, in the middle by a diagonal brace connecting the inside track frames, and in the front by an inside mounted C-frame, to which the 24-foot universal bulldozer blade was attached. The G model weighed 188,600 pounds, while the H unit tipped the scales at 183,900 pounds. Production ended on the SxS D9H in 1977. ECO

to the D7; and the RD-8 became the D8. All of these models were the same as their predecessors mechanically, including the prefix codes; only the nomenclature was different. Added to the product line in 1938 was the Caterpillar D2 (3J and 4J). This scrappy little diesel crawler was the counterpart to the Model R-2 gas tractor. In 1947, an improved D2 (4U and 5U) was released.

In the early 1940s, new model releases almost came to a halt. Not because there was anything wrong with the Caterpillar crawlers, which there wasn't, but because all current production was needed for the war effort in Europe and the Pacific.

Uncle Sam needed all of the tractors he could lay his hands on for World War II.

The Last Fifty Years

After the war, the demand for Caterpillar crawler-tractors was on the rise. Contractors that made due with whatever they had now needed new equipment as fast as they could get it. Most of these machines were delivered as dozers, instead of just plain crawler-tractors. The bulldozer blade options for Cat machines had always been available, but in the mid-1930s and early 1940s an alliance with R. G. LeTourneau, dating back to late

1934, increased the popularity of the option considerably. After this partnership ended in February 1944, Caterpillar announced in May 1944 that they were going to design and market their own types of bulldozing blades, controls, and rippers. The company's first blades were delivered in 1945, with rippers following in 1947.

Since the late 1940s, Caterpillar has introduced an incredible array of new tracked dozer models, with many variations available on several of the series marketed to a specific job function, such as logging, landfill, or wet ground conditions.

The smaller crawlers offered by Caterpillar in this time period include the D2, D3, and D4. The

The Cat D10N replaced the D9L in the product line in 1987, but do not be confused by the designation as it is not a replacement for the much larger D10. The D10N (2YD) was powered by a Cat 3412 diesel engine, rated at 557 gross horsepower and 520 fhp. Width of the "U" blade was 17 feet, 3 inches, with an earth-moving capacity of 28.7 cubic yards. Overall weight, including ripper, was 148,854 pounds. The D10N was replaced by the D10R in 1996. ECO

Caterpillar D2 series, originally dating back to 1938, was offered for the final time in 1957, ending the model line. The D3 was introduced in 1972 and was in production until 1979. Other models in the series included the D3B (1979–87); the D3C (1987–90); the D3C Series II (1990–93); and the D3C Series III (1993–). The original D4 from 1938 lasted until 1959. This was followed by the D4C (1959–63); the D4D (1963–77); the D4E (1977–84); the D4H (1985–96); the D4C Series II (1990–93); and the D4C Series III (1993–).

The Caterpillar D5 and D6 fall into the mid-size range of crawler-tractors produced by the company. The Cat D5 was first introduced in late 1966 and ran until 1977. Subsequent models included the D5B (1977–84); the D5C (1991–93); the D5H (1985–96); D5C Series III (1993–); and the D5M XL (1996–). The original Cat D6 dates back to 1938 and continued on until 1959 with various updates made along the way. This series was followed by the D6B (1959–67); the D6C (1963–1977); the D6D (1977–86); the D6H (1985–96); and the D6R (1996–).

Introduced in late-1977, the Cat D10 (84W/76X) became the benchmark in the industry. With its elevated final-drive sprocket design, it looked like no other large production machine previously produced. Power was supplied by a V-12 Cat D348 turbocharged and aftercooled diesel engine rated at 700 fhp. The largest blade offered for the D10 was a 10U Bulldozer, which was 19-feet, 8- inches wide and rated at 38.2 cubic yards. Overall working weight of a fully optioned dozer, with single shank ripper, was 190,117 pounds. Urs Peyer

The D10 model was replaced in 1986 by an even more powerful dozer—the Cat D11N. The D11N (74Z) featured a new Cat 3508, V-8 diesel engine rated at 817 gross horsepower and 770 fhp. With more power came a larger blade, and the 11U Bulldozer measured 20-feet, 10-inches across, and was rated at 45-cubic yards capacity. This D11N is equipped with the massive Cat Impact Ripper, which delivered powerful impulses to fracture rock before ripping through it. Weight of a D11N, with the impact ripper, was a meaty 225,861 pounds. **Urs Peyer**

The large dozer class of Caterpillar has been represented for years by the Cat D7, D8, and D9 models. The original D7 hit the dirt in 1938 and continued until 1955 with no less than seven different variations released during that time period. The D7C (1955–59); the D7D (1959–61); the D7E (1961–69); D7F (1969–74); the D7G (1975–86); the D7H (1986–96); and the D7R (1996–) followed the original. The Cat D8 entered service in 1938 and continued until 1955 with five tractor update variations. Additional models included the D8D, E, and F (1955–57); the D8H (1958–74); the D8K (1974–82); the D8L (1982–92); the D8N (1987–95); and the D8R (1995–).

Of the largest "low-tracked" Caterpillar dozers, the D9 is probably one of the most famous crawler-tractors in the world. The first experimental proto-type, the D9X, started field trials in 1954. Full production of the D9D started in 1955, which was replaced by the D9E in 1959. Other D9 models include the D9G (1961–74); the D9H (1974–81); the D9L (1980–86); the D9N (1987–95); and the D9R (1995–). The D9N series was not an upgraded D9H, but was derived from the D8L dozer. Even though the D9N had taken the D8L's place in the U.S. product line, the D8L model line continued to be built in overseas plants. It is interesting to note that the 25,000th crawler-tractor built by Caterpillar in 1988 was a D9N unit.

The D9 tractor was also available in two specialty factory-produced combinations: the quad, and the side-by-side. The push-pull quad unit, the

DD9G, was in production from late 1964 to 1974. It was replaced by the more powerful DD9H in 1974, which lasted until 1980. The side-by-side model, SxS D9G, was produced from 1969 to 1974 and its replacement, the SxS D9H, was built from 1974 to 1977.

dozer. The D10N was not the follow-up to the D10, but was in fact the upgraded D9L model. In 1996, the D10N was replaced by the D10R. It can be very confusing to tell one model from another at times. Thankfully, most of these instances are isolated cases in the Cat product line.

The first of Caterpillar's ultra-large dozers was the innovative and legendary D10. When the 700-flywheel horsepower D10 was introduced in late - 1977, it was the world's most powerful production crawler-dozer. It was also the first to feature the high-sprocket track-drive system, now a standard design on all but the smallest current Cat dozers. The elevated track design reduced the shock loads from ground contact, minimizing roller frame alignment problems and limiting the amount of debris that could damage the drive sprocket teeth. The D10 was upgraded in 1986 into the even more-powerful 770-fhp D11N, which was in service until it was replaced in March 1996 by the D11R. At first, the power output remained unchanged, but by August 1997 power was increased to 850 fhp. A special version of this large dozer, called the D11R CD Carrydozer, was unveiled in September 1996. Official production release for the 850-fhp Carrydozer was in mid-1998.

The D11R CD Carrydozer (9XR) was first introduced at the September 1996 MINExpo in Las Vegas, Nevada. This dozer concept was a further extension of the regular D11R, which replaced the D11N in early 1996. The Carrydozer is powered by a Cat 3508B diesel engine rated at 915 gross horsepower and 850 fhp. The specially designed bulldozer carries more material inside the blade curvature for maximum productivity. The blade is 22-feet wide and 9-feet high with a 57-cubic yard capacity rating. Total operating weight of the dozer is 239,550 pounds. The regular D11R (8ZR) received the Carrydozer's engine and power ratings in mid-1997. ECO

The 54-horsepower HT4 was a Cat D4 tractor, combined with a 1.25-cubic yard Trackson hydraulic "Traxcavator" loader attachment that was introduced in 1950. After Caterpillar bought the Trackson company in December 1951, the HT4 (35C) became a separate model type in 1952 and was produced until 1955. Pictured is a 1953 vintage model belonging to the Historical Construction Equipment Association of Grand Rapids, Ohio. ECO

The Track-type Loaders

Caterpillar entered the track-type front-end loader market in December 1951, after it had purchased the Trackson Company of Milwaukee, Wisconsin. Established in 1922, Trackson started supplying various attachments to Caterpillar, such as pipe-laying equipment in 1936, and first provided a shovel front-end option for the Model Thirty in 1937. Over the years, Trackson provided "Traxcavator" vertical-lift cable-operated, front-loading shovel attachments to early Cat D2 (T2), D4 (T4), D6 (T6), and D7 (T7) crawler-tractors. In 1950, a hydraulic Traxcavator option was added to the Cat D4, making it the Model HT4, which stayed in production until 1955. After

Caterpillar's largest track-type loader was its 983 series, first introduced in 1969. The 983 (38K) was powered by a Cat D343, six-cylinder diesel engine, rated at 275 fhp. Bucket capacity was five cubic yards. Overall working weight, with ROPS cab and ripper, was 80,170 pounds. The 983 was upgraded into the 983B (58X) model in 1978, featuring the Cat 3406 diesel engine and improved ROPS cab. Power remained unchanged, but the weight increased to 82,751 pounds with ripper. Production ended in 1982. Urs Peyer

the Caterpillar purchase, other various older-design shovels, such as the Model LW2 and L2, continued to be offered for a short time. But in late-1952, Caterpillar introduced the Model No. 6 Traxcavator, the company's first track-type tractor-shovel that was built from the ground up with the loader addition being an integrated design element and not just an add-on attachment. The model was an instant success and opened another chapter in Caterpillar history.

Caterpillar has produced numerous models and variations of track-type loaders over the years. Initial model introductions of front-engined machines include the Caterpillar 931 in 1972; the 933C in 1955; the 939 in 1993; the 941 in 1968; the 951 in 1964; the 955C in 1955; the 977D in 1955; and the 983 in 1969. Rear-engined, hydrostatic drive models include the 943 in 1980; the 953 and 963 in 1981; and the 973 in 1982.

Caterpillar replaced the 983B series with the new hydrostatic drive, rear-engined 973 Track Loader, which was first introduced in late 1981 as a 1982 model. The 973 (26Z/32Z) is powered by a Cat 3306 diesel engine rated at 229 gross horsepower and 210 fhp. Bucket capacity is 4.2 cubic yards with an average operating weight of 55,196 pounds without ripper, and 57,903 pounds with it. Caterpillar, Inc.

CHAPTER 3

The Motor Graders

In the history of Caterpillar earthmoving equipment, the motor graders are the second oldest product line, after the crawler-tractors, still built by the company in the present day. What the motor grader (also known as a road grader or blade grader) lacks in dynamic presence while in operation, it more than makes up for its in ability to do precise grading work on all types of roadway systems. Some of its work duties include windrowing, ditching, scarifying (ripping), snow removal, mine haul road maintenance, and all manner of road edging and fine grading.

The history of the Cat grader line can be traced back directly to a company called the Russell Grading Manufacturing Co. This company was founded in 1903 by Richard Russell and C. K. Stockland in

Caterpillar released the earth-moving industry's first true production motor grader in 1931, called the Auto Patrol. The grader's overall design with its high-mounted rear engine, was a single unit, not an individual tractor with a separate front-end attachment. This Auto Patrol, pictured in 1931, is one of the first few built. Caterpillar, Inc.

This No. 12 (9K) still looks good after many long years of service. This particular model of the No. 12 motor grader was produced from 1938 to 1945. It was powered by a Cat diesel engine rated at 70 horsepower, and carried a 12-foot-wide moldboard—perfect for secondary and rural road work. The overall design of this early mechanically controlled model is not all that different from today's modern hydraulic machines. ECO

Stephen, Minnesota. The Russell Company's first major product release was a horse-drawn elevating type of grader, with a gas-engine-driven conveyer. In the beginning, the building of the new machine was farmed-out to the makers of the conveyor system, but to help control the grader's cost, all manufacturing was brought in-house in 1906. After additional financing was secured, a new factory location was found in Minneapolis, Minnesota, which greatly increased the company's manufacturing capabilities.

The financial troubles and delays encountered in the development of the elevating grader were offset by Russell's other product offerings, which included blade graders, drag and wheel scrapers, and plows. The first of these, a small two-horse road maintenance grader, was introduced in 1908. After this came the first eight-horse-pulled Simplex Road Machine, followed by the Traction Special, a grader specifically built for use with a tractor, both also in 1908. Other popular Russell blade graders would soon emerge, carrying such names as the Standard

(1912); the Mogul (1913); the Super-Mogul (1922); the Reliance (1915); the Super-Reliance (1923); the Special (1912); and the Super-Special (1924). All were designed to be pulled by a tractor.

The next evolutionary step in the Russell line happened in 1919, when the company produced its first prototype self-propelled grader. The machine consisted of a two-wheel Allis-Chalmers tractor in the front with the grader portion of the unit in the rear. This concept would officially be introduced in 1920 as the Russell Motor Hi-Way Patrol No. 1. Interest in the marketplace was high, but when Allis-Chalmers ran into patent violation problems with that particular tractor model, it had to be withdrawn from the market. This caused Russell's self-propelled grader to be put on hold, but only for a short time.

In 1925, Russell released a newly designed self-propelled model that used the tractor portion in the rear, with the grader in the front. This new model, the Motor Patrol No. 2, utilized a Fordson tractor and was in production until 1928. Introduced in late 1925, the

Motor Patrol No. 3 was based on McCormick-Deering's Model 10-20, and was in production until 1929. Motor Patrol No. 4 was in production from late 1926 to 1929 and was based on a Caterpillar Two-Ton crawler-tractor. In 1927, Motor Patrol No. 5 was offered with a Cletrac K-20 crawler-tractor, but only lasted until 1929. And in 1928, the Motor Patrol No. 6 came out, based on the Caterpillar Twenty.

The success of this type of motor grader was not lost on the industry, and especially not at the Caterpillar Tractor Co. The popularity of the Russell Motor Patrol No. 4, utilizing the Cat Two-Ton tractor, had convinced company officials that the Russell grader product line needed a new home. After some early meetings between the two companies, a deal was formally reached in August 1928 in which Caterpillar would purchase the entire Russell Grader Manufacturing Co. At first, many of the blade and elevating graders joined the Cat product line unchanged. Motor Patrol models that utilized

a competitor's tractor were naturally discontinued. The new Caterpillar self-propelled graders would consist of the Motor Patrol Model No. 10 with a Cat Ten tractor (1929); the Model No. 15 with the Cat Fifteen (1929); and the Model No. 20 with the Cat Twenty, which was formerly known as a Motor Patrol No. 6 (1928).

The old-fashioned tractor-pulled graders still had a good customer base in the marketplace, so Caterpillar freshened up the old Russell designs with the release of four new grader model introductions. These were the Cat No. 77 (also known as the Cat Sixty Leaning Wheel Grader) in 1930; the No. 66 (Fifty Leaning Wheel) in 1932; the No. 44 (Thirty or Thirty-Five Leaning Wheel) in 1930; and the No. 33 (Twenty or Twenty-Five Leaning Wheel) in 1931.

But the real change was in the company's self-propelled grader concept as a whole. In 1931, Caterpillar introduced the new "Auto Patrol," the industry's first, true production motor grader. Unlike the

Caterpillar offered the No. 16 (49G), its first motor grader with hydraulic-mechanical controls, in early-1963. This was replaced by the fully hydraulic Model 16G (93U) in 1973. The earth-moving industry waited until late 1994 for the upgraded 16H to be released. The 16H is powered by a Cat 3406 diesel engine rated at 288 gross horsepower and 275 fhp. The moldboard length is 16 feet, which is the same as all other Cat 16 motor graders before it. ECO

The Caterpillar 24H is the largest motor grader ever produced by the company, and is also the largest currently available to the industry. The big grader is powered by a Cat 3412E twelve-cylinder, turbocharged diesel engine rated at 540 gross horsepower and 500 fhp. The moldboard blade is 24-feet wide and 42-inches high. Here it is working in a Wyoming coal mine in the Powder River Basin. It was the first 24H shipped to a customer in early 1996. ECO

earlier Motor Patrols, where the grader was simply a front-end attachment to an existing crawler unit, the revolutionary Auto Patrol had its own engine placed high and in the rear of the machine. This kept the engine in a cleaner work environment, improved operator visibility, and increased traction on the drive-axle. This design would be the basis for all motor graders to come. Competitors were quick to recognize the advantages of this layout and immediately started to redesign their own grader offerings.

Different early models offered by Caterpillar were the Auto Patrol No. 9 in 1931; the No. 7 in 1932; the very popular No. 11 in 1932; and the No. 10 in 1933. Early Cat grader models utilized gas-powered engines. But in 1934, a Diesel Auto Patrol was offered, enabling customers to chose the engine type that suited them best. All of these models had only a single rear-drive axle, but by late 1934 both of the current models, the No. 10 and 11, were offered with single or tandem rear-drive axles. Tandem-axles helped relieve the bouncing or "loping" ride that the single rear-axle graders commonly suffered from.

In 1938, the company released its most popular and famous motor grader of all time—the incredible Cat No. 12. Key to the No. 12's design was its triple-box section main frame, which was stronger and far more rigid than that of the old No. 11's twin-beam design. This layout established the look of all modern Cat motor graders to this very day. The No. 12 was powered by a Cat diesel engine. Two different starting options were available for the No. 12 diesel. It could be ordered with a push-button, direct electric start system, or with a small, built-in gasoline engine (often referred to as a "pony motor") to crank the engine over. All models in this series utilized tandem rear-drive axles. By 1965, the No. 12F was offered with hydraulically-actuated mechanical blade controls, making operation much easier. All controls became fully hydraulic with the No. 12G grader, introduced in 1973. The series was still available in 1998, as the Cat 12H Motor Grader (which was first released in 1995) making it the longest-running production model in the grader product line, with over 60 years of service.

The 24H has a standard three-shank D6-sized ripper with the capacity for a total of seven shanks. The grader is 51-feet, 10-inches in length and has a maximum overall working weight of 130,902 pounds. The 24H shown here is equipped with the wider wheel and tire option, with the rear fenders removed. ECO

Other Cat motor grader models introduced around the time of the original No. 12 were the No. 112 and the No. 212, both in 1939. Looking much like a No. 12 model, these units had less power. In addition to both models using tandem-drive axles, the No. 112 was also briefly offered in a single-drive version. The smaller No. 212 was also offered with single-drive well into the early 1950s.

Caterpillar has offered many different models of motor graders in its product line over the years. Some of these include the Cat 120 series in 1964; the 130G series in 1973; the 140 series in 1970; the all-wheel-drive 143H series in 1995; the No. 14B series in 1959; the 160G series in 1986; the all-wheel-drive 163H series in 1995; and the very popular No. 16 series in early 1963. The No. 16 grader was the first of Caterpillar's machines to offer hydraulic-mechanical blade controls.

The largest grader to be designed and built by Caterpillar is the massive 24H Motor Grader. This extremely large piece of equipment actually got its start back in 1987 at Caterpillar's then-new Mining Vehicle Center (MVC) at the Decatur, Illinois, plant. At that time, the large motor grader project was classified as the 18H series. But after development had started, projections concerning where the market was going for this size of machine had

increased. The 18H concept soon evolved into the even larger 24H, which was officially introduced in early 1996. The 24H grader was designed for use in mining operations where larger haul roads are required. As the cost of the trucks and their tires continues to rise, haul roads need to be widened, cleaned, and groomed in such a way that they do not effect the haulers. Debris in the haul road can easily cause tire cuts and side-wall punctures. This can be very expensive, especially when one considers that each of the larger-sized tires costs in the neighborhood of $30,000! The Cat 24H is currently the world's largest full-production motor grader. Larger machines have been offered in the past, from such firms as Champion, RayGo, and Acco, but all were either limited production or experimental.

When Caterpillar entered this market in 1928, its principal rivals at the time were firms with names like Adams, Galion, Austin and Western, Huber, and Riddell (Warco). Today, most of these companies have vanished or have been absorbed by other manufacturers. Today's competition comes mainly from companies such as Komatsu (Galion), Volvo/Champion, and John Deere. The one constant through these last 70 years has been that Caterpillar road graders have always been Caterpillar. Period.

CHAPTER 4

The Scrapers

In the 1930s and early 1940s, the Caterpillar Tractor Company depended on various outside companies to supply pull-type scrapers for use with its crawler-tractors. As with the bulldozing blades and controls, R. G. LeTourneau manufactured a large assortment of pull-type scrapers that were sold through Caterpillar dealers nationwide. This alliance between the two companies would come to a sudden halt in mid-1944 when Caterpillar announced that it was going to start production on a new line of scrapers designed in-house, by the company.

Back in late 1940, Caterpillar started in the direction of independence from some of its long-time allied suppliers with the introduction of the Cat DW10 (1N) Tractor. The DW10 was a 90-horse-

The No. 463F tractor-drawn scraper is pulled by a D9G crawler in this photo. The No. 463F (62C) was rated at 21-cubic yards struck and 28 heaped and was in production until 1971. The No. 463 series of scrapers was originally introduced in 1955 as a replacement for the Cat No. 90 unit. ECO

Officially released in 1951, the Caterpillar DW21 was the company's first two-wheel tractor-pulled scraper. The DW21 (8W) was powered by a Cat diesel six-cylinder engine, rated at 275 gross horsepower and 225 fhp. Standard scraper capacity was 15-cubic yards struck and 20 heaped. Pictured being push-loaded by a Cat D9D in 1957 is a 300-fhp DW21C (58C), with a No. 470 (69C) scraper unit. Capacity was up to 18-cubic yards struck and 25 heaped. ECO collection

power diesel-engined, two-axle, four-wheel, rear-wheel-drive tractor designed for high speed earth-moving work, either by pulling a scraper or a Cat-designed W10 bottom-dump wagon. The DW10 was often found matched to various builds of scraper units including the CW-10 Carrymor LaPlant-Choate model, and especially the R. G. LeTourneau Carryall Model LS. The DW10's design was rather sleek for its day, at least as far as earth-moving equipment was concerned. Its rounded front fenders and radiator shroud were more in keeping with designs found in the over-the-road trucks then in use. The DW10 proved to be a tough little tractor in the field. All it needed was a Cat-designed scraper behind it.

Caterpillar introduced the No. 70 and No. 80 Scrapers as its first tractor-towed scraper models in

early 1946. These were followed by the No. 60 in 1947, the No. 40 in 1949, and the No. 90 in 1951. These towed scrapers were matched to the following Cat crawler-tractors: the No. 40 was for a D4; the No. 60 teamed up with a D6; the No. 70 was meant for a D7; and the larger No. 80 and No. 90 units got the more powerful D8. The Cat No. 10 scraper from 1947 and the No. 20 from 1951 were meant for use behind Cat's high-speed, four-wheel tractors, the DW10 and DW20, respectively.

Starting in 1955, Caterpillar started to release upgraded models of these scrapers with new product designations. The Cat No. 463 replaced the No. 90 in 1955; the No. 435C replaced the No. 80 in 1956; and the No. 491, released in 1956, became the largest in the series. The towed scrapers remained in the Caterpillar product line until the

The Caterpillar DW20 tractor/scraper became a very popular model for the company when it was officially released in 1951. This 1960 vintage DW20G (87E), with the No. 456 (88E) scraper, has 345 fhp and demonstrates that it is still able to get the job done. The scraper unit is rated at 19.5-cubic yards struck and 27 heaped. ECO

last series produced, the model Cat 435G, was withdrawn in 1973.

Caterpillar's four-wheeled tractor-pulled scrapers got their start in 1947 with the release of the Cat DW10 tractor and No. 10 scraper combination, as already mentioned. It was replaced by the model DW15 in 1954. The DW15 was available with both the No. 10 and new No. 15 scraper units. The older No. 10 scraper was only produced for the DW15 in its first year. In 1957, the No. 15 was upgraded into the No. 428 scraper, first available on the DW15E. The last model produced, the DW15F, ended production in 1959.

The real star in the early Caterpillar scraper product line was the tractor/scraper combination Cat DW20, introduced in 1948 with full production commencing in 1951. The early 225-flywheel horsepower diesel-engined DW20 tractors were available with the No. 20 scraper and the W20 bottom-dump wagon. In 1955, the scraper portion of the unit was replaced by the No. 456 model with the introduction of the 300-fhp DW20E. The last series, produced from 1958 to 1960, was the 345-fhp DW20G available with either the 19.5-cubic yard struck No. 456, or the larger 24-cubic yard No. 482. The DW20 series was a favorite with customers. It was a rugged, tough, and reliable machine that made a lot of money for the contractors who operated them.

Caterpillar has produced some real workhorses in the four-wheel tractor/scraper model lineup over the years. Some of these include the single-engined Cat 630A with the 482C scraper unit in 1960, and the models 632, 650, and 660, all in 1962. The largest and most powerful model built in the series was the famous tandem-powered Cat 666. First introduced

In mid-1962, Cat's largest and most powerful production scraper ever built was unveiled—the mighty tandem-powered Cat 666. The early Model 666 (77F/20G) had combined power ratings of 785 fhp for both engines. By 1964, power had gone up to 835 fhp, and then to 900 fhp in 1966. In 1969, a more powerful 666B (66K/20G) model was made available, and it was rated at 950 fhp. Capacity of the scraper unit was 40-cubic yards struck and 54-cubic yards heaped, with a maximum 128,000-pound load rating. ECO

in 1962, the model 666 had a combined maximum power rating of 980 gross horsepower (785 fhp) available from the tractor and rear scraper diesel engines. Capacity was rated at 54-cubic yards heaped and 40 struck. This was the same rating as for the model 660 rear scraper unit. In 1969, the most powerful version of this model was released as the 666B. It carried a combined power rating of 950 fhp, 550 from the front Cat eight-cylinder diesel engine and 400 from the rear six-cylinder powerplant. The last year of production for the big 666B was in 1978.

The overhung engine scraper was another type of self-propelled scraper produced by Caterpillar, but it was a two-wheel, single-axle tractor type. This type of machine was first introduced by R. G. LeTourneau

in 1938 as the Tournapull. The early Tournapulls were powered by Cat diesel engines and were sold and serviced by Caterpillar dealers. But when Caterpillar and LeTourneau parted ways in 1944, this left Cat with the task of designing and building its own rubber-tired, two-wheel tractor-pulled scraper. By 1948, Caterpillar had designed a 15-cubic yard struck capacity prototype model called the Cat DW21. This machine, more than any other, would influence the look of today's modern Cat scrapers. More important, it would help establish the company as the world leader in this market segment.

After months of field testing, the Cat DW21 was introduced in late 1950 with its cousin, the DW20. Full production started in 1951 with the

Caterpillar introduced the 627 series of wheel tractor-scrapers in 1968. The Model 627 (54K) was powered by two Cat D333 diesel engines, with a combined power rating of 450 fhp. Capacity of the scraper was 14-cubic yards struck and 20-cubic yards heaped. Today's 627F, introduced in 1993, is rated at 555 fhp. Scraper capacity has remained unchanged. ECO Collection

opening of the new Joliet Plant in Illinois. The Caterpillar DW21 was powered by a six-cylinder Cat diesel engine, rated at 275 gross horsepower and 225 fhp. The scraper unit was a No. 21 model. In 1955, a more powerful version was released, the DW21C, with an engine rating of 300 fhp. Also new was a slightly larger No. 470 scraper unit. Other models to follow were the DW21D in 1958, and the DW21G, also in 1958. The DW21G version was the last to be produced, and it was the most powerful at 345 fhp. The last year of production for the DW21G was 1960.

In 1959, Caterpillar launched all new models of its two-wheel-type tractor series of scrapers to continue the work started by the DW21. The first of these to be introduced was the Cat 619B in 1959, followed by the 631A in 1960. Other significant first model introductions include the 641,

651, and 657, all in 1962. These were followed by the 621 in 1965, the 627 in 1968, and the 637 in 1970. The Cat 627, 637, and 657 were all tandem-engine-powered models.

Caterpillar has also produced various elevator scraper model types over the years, starting with the Cat J619 in 1964. This model was based on the standard model 619 scraper, but the rear scraper bowl was equipped with an elevator loading attachment built by Johnson Manufacturing Company. However, this was only offered until 1965 when it was replaced by the Cat J621. After this model's release, all of the company's elevator-type loading scrapers were built as stand-alone model lines. These included the Cat 633 in 1966; the 613A in 1969; the 623 in 1972; and the model 639D in 1979. The Cat 639D was the most powerful elevator-type wheel tractor-scraper, factory-produced by the company.

Introduced in 1962, the Caterpillar 641 (64F) was a good performer on the job site. The 641 was powered by a single eight-cylinder Cat diesel engine, rated at 450 fhp. Capacity for the scraper unit was 28-cubic yards struck and 38 heaped. The model was upgraded to the 641B (65K) in 1969 with an increased power output of 550 fhp. Production ended on the series in 1981. Urs Peyer

The 657E, introduced in late 1982, is Cat's largest wheel-type scraper as of 1998. The unit pictured is a push-pull 657E (91Z/87Z) powered by a Cat 3412E diesel engine in the front tractor, and a Cat 3408E in the rear scraper. Combined power output for both units is 950 fhp. Capacity is 32-cubic yards struck and 44 heaped. ECO

It was the only one that utilized tandem engines, producing a combined 700 fhp. Load capacity of the 639D was the same as that of the later model 633D, 34-cubic yards heaped. All of Caterpillar's factory-built machines utilized hydraulic motor driven elevators in the scraper units.

The popularity of the large tractor wheel-scrapers peaked in the 1970s earth-moving industry. Since then, many manufacturers have discontinued building these types of machines. Many factors come into play when explaining why this has happened, such as job sizes, the initial high costs of the units, and a large factor is the switch to articulated haulers and hydraulic excavators. This equipment match-up is able to do the same job for which many of these scrapers were designed. The contractor also has the ability to assign the truck and excavator to other specific working applications, thus utilizing their equipment purchases to the fullest. But when it comes to transporting the material over a longer distance, then the wheel tractor-scrapers' performance still makes it the top choice.

The Caterpillar 633 (86H) elevating-scraper was first introduced in 1966 and looked like the unit pictured here working in 1969. Its Cat diesel engine produced 400 fhp, with a scraper capacity of 32-cubic yards heaped. Currently, the 633E (1EB), introduced in 1993, is the largest elevator-type unit offered by the company, with power ratings of 490 fhp and a 34-cubic yard heaped capacity. ECO Collection

CHAPTER 5

The Wheel Loaders, Dozers, and Backhoes

The front-end wheel loader is probably one of the most versatile and prevalent pieces of equipment in use today. Typically, they are seen working along the roadway, cleaning up debris, moving material on a construction site (from houses to skyscrapers), loading trucks in a quarry, or operating in large mining complexes. You name it, the wheel loader is there.

Caterpillar entered the front-end wheel loader market in 1959. The company was not the first to produce this type of machine. Manufacturers such as Hough and Clark Michigan already produced proven and popular product lines of these types of loaders. Caterpillar had its popular

The No. 944A "Traxcavator" was the first rubber-tired front-end loader to be built by Caterpillar. The No. 944A (43A) was released in 1959 and was powered by either a Cat D330 diesel engine, or by an optional gasoline unit. Both were rated at 105 fhp, and bucket capacity was 2 cubic yards. The No. 944A was a rigid frame type and steered with its rear wheels. Production ended in 1968. Caterpillar, Inc.

The model 988 (87A) was the first articulated steering wheel loader to be released by Caterpillar in early 1963. Power was supplied by a Cat D343 diesel engine, rated at 300 fhp. Bucket capacity was 5 cubic yards. The current 1998 Cat 988F Series II loader is rated at 430 fhp with a 8- to 9-cubic yard capacity bucket range. Urs Peyer

tracked "Traxcavator" front-end loaders, but the new rubber-tired-loader markets could not be ignored.

The first model to be introduced by Caterpillar was the No. 944A Traxcavator. The No. 944A carried a 2-cubic yard capacity bucket and was powered by either a Cat diesel or a regular gasoline engine. Next to follow, in 1960, was the smaller 1.25-cubic yard No. 922A, and the larger 2.75-cubic yard No. 966A. Both of these units were also classified as a "Wheel-type Traxcavator" in the product line. All of these machines had a rigid frame and steered with their rear wheels. But a new type of machine was just around the corner that promised

greater performance and maneuverability than any loader in service at the time. It would be the articulated wheel loader.

The articulated steering design was first introduced by Scoopmobile in 1953, but technical difficulties delayed production of any serious numbers until the late 1950s. Even though the engineering designs of articulated steering were sound and carried considerable merit, it would take a few years of testing by various manufacturers to get the bugs worked out. And work them out they did.

Caterpillar first introduced two new models of articulated wheel loaders into the marketplace.

The most famous of all Cat loaders are the 992 series of machines. First introduced in 1968, the 992 (25K) was powered by a V-12 Cat D348 diesel engine rated at 550 fhp. The 992 (pictured working in 1969) clearly shows what a fully loaded 10-cubic yard bucket looks like. ECO collection

These were the new 5-cubic yard Cat 988 in early 1963, and the redesigned 966B in mid-1963. Like earlier Cat offerings, these machines were classified as "Traxcavators." But confusion among buyers as to which models had tracks and which had rubber tires was very irritating to the company. By the end of 1965, the Traxcavator name was dropped from the rubber-tired loader program. From then on, they would be referred to as simply wheel loaders.

At Caterpillar, wheel loader development was put into high gear. In late 1965, the company introduced the very popular 4-cubic yard Cat 980. This was followed by the release of the models 950 and 992, both in 1968. The Cat 992 series is considered one of the greatest large wheel-loader designs ever produced. It has been the best-selling machine in its class size since it was introduced, and by a considerable margin. The 992, when it was initially

The Cat 992 was upgraded to the 992B (25K) model series in 1973. The biggest visual difference between the two models is the pin-on ROPS cab on the 992B version. The 992B was replaced in 1977 by the more powerful 690-fhp Cat 992C (42X). ECO

Caterpillar's revolutionary 992G wheel loader was introduced at the 1996 MINExpo in Las Vegas as the forthcoming replacement for the 710-fhp Cat 992D model. The 992G loader's special design is its one-piece, cast-steel, box-section front lift arm. The Cat 3508B EUI diesel engine developing 800 fhp powers the loader. Bucket capacity ranges from 15- to 16- cubic yards. Overall working weight is 201,982 pounds, or 101 tons. ECO

The very contemporary-looking Caterpillar 980G wheel loader was introduced in 1995 as a replacement for the 980F Series II. The 980G is powered by a 300-fhp Cat 3406C DITA diesel engine. Bucket capacity ranges from 5- to 7.5- cubic yards. The 980 loader series has been offered by Caterpillar since late 1965. Urs Peyer

As of 1998, the Caterpillar 994 is the largest wheel loader ever offered by the company. First introduced in 1990, the 994 (9YF) is powered by a sixteen-cylinder Cat 3516 diesel engine that cranks out a whopping 1,250 fhp. Standard bucket size is 23 cubic yards with a 70,000-pound capacity rating. The special chains on the front tires help protect them from severe rock cuts and abrasions. Each tire chain costs about $30,000 per wheel. ECO

At 390,300 pounds, the Cat 994 is a colossal machine. This 994, pictured working in a Wyoming coal mine, was the first equipped with a 45-cubic yard coal bucket in 1995 for loading the lighter-weight and larger-volume material. It can load a high-sided 190-ton coal hauler in six passes, which takes about three minutes. ECO

released, was classified as a 10-cubic yard machine. With the introduction of the 992C in 1977, bucket capacity had increased to 12.5 cubic yards. The 992D model of 1992 raised the capacity to 14 cubic yards, and today's revolutionary 992G wheel loader, which was unveiled in late 1996, is rated as a 15- to 16-cubic yard machine.

Other popular Caterpillar wheel loader model lines to be introduced over the years have included the Cat 910 in 1973; the 914G in 1995; the 916 in 1986; the 918F in 1992; the 920 in 1969; the 926 in 1984; the 928F in 1993; the 930 in 1968; the 936 in 1983; the 938F in 1994; and the large 990 in 1993.

The latest models introduced in 1998 include the Cat 950G, 966G, 962G, and the 972G. The introduction of the new 966G continues an unbroken line of more than 38 years that the 966 series has been offered by Caterpillar, the longest of any wheel loader in its product line.

Of all of the wheel loaders built by Caterpillar since 1959, none can compare in size or capacity to the massive Cat 994. The 994 model is almost twice as large as the next Cat loader offering, the 992, and was designed primarily for large-scale mining operations. The loader is powered by a single Cat 3516 diesel engine, rated at 1,336 gross horsepower and 1,250 fhp. The 994's drivetrain is all mechanical, while its closest competition from LeTourneau, Inc. is diesel-electric drive. Standard rock bucket capacity for the 994 is 23 cubic yards. Overall working weight of the big loader is 390,300 pounds, or 195 tons. The next in line, 992G, weighs in at 101 tons.

A close cousin to the wheel loaders in the Caterpillar product line are the articulated rubber-tired wheel dozers. The first of these to be introduced were the Cat 824 and 834 models, both in early 1963. In 1970, the 814, a third smaller model, was released. The high-speed nature of the wheel dozers made them a versatile production tool when it came to push-loading scrapers, coal stockpiling, and mine pit floor clean-up around the loading areas of the large shovels.

Introduced in early 1963, the Caterpillar 834 wheel-type tractor dozer was the largest version offered by the company until the purchase of the two larger Tiger wheel dozer model lines in 1997. The 834 (43E) was originally powered by a 360-fhp Cat D343 diesel engine, which was later increased to 400 fhp. Between 1974 and 1982, the 834 was dropped from production. In 1982, a 450-fhp Model 834B (92Z) dozer was introduced and, as of 1998, it is still offered in the product line. Urs Peyer

Caterpillar had previously released a tractor-type wheel dozer in late 1956, the Cat No. 668 Series C. The No. 668 unit was based on the Cat DW20 tractor used in scraper applications. Success of this model was very limited, and few were built.

Included in the same family group as the wheel dozers are the soil compactors. Very similar to their rubber-tired counterparts, the compactors are equipped with metal wheels, studded with multiple steel tamping feet. These serve the same function as a tractor-pulled sheepsfoot drum roller. Models

produced by Caterpillar include the Cat 815, 825B, and 835 series, all introduced in 1970. Landfill versions of the soil compactors include the Cat 816 and 826B, released in 1972, and the 836, which was introduced in 1993.

A very competitive class of machines in the construction marketplace are the backhoe loaders. For years, these versatile tractors, with a front-loading bucket and a rear hydraulic excavator-type backhoe attachment, have been produced by the big manufacturers in farm implement production, such as

The front-engined Caterpillar 830M wheel-dozer was a special military model not offered as a regular production model, and was first delivered into active service in 1962. The 830M (41E) had the same engine as that found in the Cat 834, but developed 357 fhp (830MB rating only). Today, many of these wheel-tractors are painted yellow and sold off as army surplus, like the unit shown. Urs Peyer

The Caterpillar 835 (44N) was the largest construction compactor ever offered by the company. First released in 1970, it utilized the same 400-fhp engine found in the 834 dozer. The unit shown is equipped with rock-tamper steel wheels, best suited for crushing and compacting rock fills. The Cat 835 was dropped from the product line in 1974. Urs Peyer

John Deere, Case, and Ford. Add to these fine machines the products built by JCB in England and you have one extremely difficult market segment to break into. But as in times past, Caterpillar was ready to roll up its sleeves and take on the established manufacturers with all-new backhoe loader designs of its own.

Caterpillar released its first backhoe loader in 1985, as the Cat 416. This was followed by the models 426 and 428 in 1986; the 436 and 438 in 1988; and the largest in the lineup, the 446, in 1989. It did not take long for Caterpillar to establish itself in this marketplace, and is now considered one of the top builders of backhoe loaders in the world today.

Officially introduced in early 1996, the Caterpillar 436C backhoe loader is one very sophisticated piece of earth-moving equipment. It offers an advanced 85-fhp Cat 3054T turbocharged diesel engine. The loader also incorporates full hydrostatic all-wheel steering, and a special box section backhoe boom design for superior strength and balance. Caterpillar, Inc.

CHAPTER 6

The Haulers

Caterpillar was slow to enter the off-road hauler market. This segment of the industry was already occupied by some very well-established manufacturers, such as Dart, Mack, and Euclid. In the late 1950s, other companies like LeTourneau-Westinghouse, Autocar, and Kenworth were also entering the off-road market. The playing field was very crowded when Caterpillar decided to enter the fray, but cries from its dealerships for a true quarry and mining truck to round out the Cat product line had to be answered. Also, future projections for sales of off-road haulers were very high, with additional manufacturers ready to jump in with new diesel-electric drive trucks. The time was right for Caterpillar to show the industry

The most popular 100-ton capacity hauler on the market today is the Caterpillar 777D, which was introduced in early 1996 as the replacement for the previous 777C version. Power is supplied by a Cat 3508B EUI diesel rated at 938 fhp. The 777D (3PR) heritage dates back to 1974 when the first Cat 777 (84A) was introduced. ECO

61

just how an off-road, rear-dump truck should be designed and built.

In 1962, Caterpillar officially introduced its newest creation—the 769. The 35-ton-capacity 769 was an entirely new design—not based on some existing machine platform already in production. The truck design was unique with the familiar Cat radiator grille up front and a Cat diesel engine under the hood, so to speak. The design utilized many rounded-off corners around the radiator shroud, fuel tank, and upper decking. The 769 also incorporated an offset cab on the left, which shortened the length of the front end, as opposed to the long-nosed designs of the Euclid haulers of the time. The scrappy little hauler was a winner from the get-go and it was now off to bigger and better things, or at least that was the plan.

When the 769 was released, the industry was starting to take a more·serious look at larger capacity, diesel-electric drive trucks. In these types of haulers, the diesel engine powers a generator, which provides the necessary current to drive the electric motors, either mounted in the axle housing or directly in the wheel itself. This eliminated the need for a mechanical transmission and driveshaft. Already, manufacturers such as Unit Rig, WABCO, and, to a certain extent, Dart were releasing, or were about to release, diesel-electric drive models in the 75- to 100-ton capacity range. To counter this, Caterpillar started development of its own line of diesel-electric haulers, with designs finalized by 1964.

During 1965, three new Cat trucks started rigorous proving-ground and job-site testing. These Cat diesel-electric drive haulers—the two-axle 779, the three-axle 783, and the massive 786 coal hauler—were all designed concurrently, to maximize usage of shared components. All three models utilized a newly designed Caterpillar D348 twelve-cylinder diesel engine, rated at 1,000 gross horsepower and 960 fhp at 2,000 rpm, powering a Cat-designed electrical drive system. In the case of the 786, two engines were used, one on either end of the unit.

The 240-ton capacity Caterpillar 786 coal hauler was the first experimental prototype diesel-electric drive. It is pictured here at its introduction in October 1965. The 786 (1A) utilized two tractors, one at either end, each with its own Cat D348 V-12 diesel engine developing 1,000 gross horsepower and 960 fhp, for a total of 2,000 gross horsepower and 1,920 fhp. Power was supplied to each of the tractor's leading axles through twin Caterpillar-designed electric drive systems. Caterpillar, Inc.

In 1962, Caterpillar designed and built its first off-road, rear-dump hauler, which was called the Model 769. The Cat 769 (99F) was powered by a Cat D343 diesel engine, developing 375 fhp. By 1965, this figure had risen to 400 fhp. Load capacity for the 769 was 35 tons. Urs Peyer

The rear-dump Caterpillar 779 was originally rated as a 75-ton capacity hauler when it first entered prototype testing, but by the time the first production 779 was delivered into service in 1967, the capacity had increased to 85 tons.

The 779 did make it into limited production, but after 1969, Cat management decided that the future development of diesel-electric drive trucks did not fit into its long-range plans and had the entire program canceled. Cat reacquired all of the 779 haulers working in the marketplace and had them all dismantled, thus ending any need to supply parts or support warranties on the diesel-electric-driven trucks.

The Caterpillar 783 was a three-axle design that steered with its front and rear axles. Only the center axle was powered. Also unique to this truck was its side-dumping box, rated at 100-ton capacity, but at least one rear-dump version was also built and tested. This experimental hauler was unveiled to the industry at the October 1965 AMC (American Mining Congress) Mining Show in Las Vegas. After

further testing of the 783 concept, Caterpillar decided not to pursue a production version and the program was canceled.

The 786, with its 240-ton capacity, was the largest of the three Cat diesel-electric drive haulers, and was, in fact, the largest hauler of any kind in the world when it was introduced in October 1965. It was designed as a shuttle-type of bottom-dump coal hauler, enabling the hauler to work in very restricted areas. The 786 had duel cabs and engines, one at each end of the unit. This allowed the operators to pull the 786 straight into a loading situation and then come out the way they came in, without ever turning around. Depending on which cab the operator was driving from, that would then be the front end of the unit. In total, one prototype and four preproduction 786 haulers were built, with the last four units having slightly redesigned tractor units, as compared to the original prototype from 1965. The five 786 coal haulers worked very well in service, but were parked in the early 1970s

Introduced in late 1966, the Cat 769B (99F) replaced the original 769 hauler with many new improvements. Some of these new developments included more power with 415 fhp now available, a new "V" bottom design dump body, a larger tire option, and an improved cab. The 769B ceased production in 1978 after it was replaced by the upgraded 769C (1X) series. Urs Peyer

The Caterpillar 777 model line was the next to follow in 1974. This truck sported a new design with a squared-off radiator front end and new cab, and a hauler capacity of 85 tons.

The 769, 773, and 777 model lines carried the load for Caterpillar in its truck product lineup until the mid-1980s, when larger mining-sized haulers were introduced. Today, all three of the company's original mechanical drive haulers are still offered, carrying bigger loads and offering more power and sophistication. This kind of efficiency was nearly impossible to fathom in the 1960s. The 769B was upgraded to the 769C model in 1978, and then to

when Cat canceled the electric drive program. By the mid-1980s, the last remnants of the 786 trucks still sitting in the Captain Mine's bone yard in Illinois, where the haulers had spent their entire working lives, were scrapped. Today, nothing remains of any of these fantastic creations, including the smaller 779 and 783 models. From this point on, all Caterpillar trucks would be of a mechanical drive nature, and they have been this way ever since.

In 1970, Caterpillar released its second truck in its conventional hauler product line, the 773. The 773 joined Cat's other truck, the 769B, which had been upgraded in 1966 as the one, two punch in the Cat rear-dump lineup.

The 773 looked very similar to its little brother, only larger. It was classified as a 50-ton capacity hauler. As with the 769 model, the 773 series proved to be very successful for Caterpillar.

In early 1970, the second all-mechanical-drive hauler, the 773, joined the company's lineup. Looking much like the smaller 769, the Model 773 (63G) was powered by a Cat 600-fhp D346 diesel engine. A more powerful 650-fhp Cat 773B (63W) replaced the 773 in 1978. Load capacity for the hauler was 50 tons. Urs Peyer

the 769D in 1995. The 773 was replaced by the 773B in 1978, and then by the 773D in 1996. The popular 777 was upgraded to the 777B in 1985; a 777C in 1991; and then into the 777D in 1996. By this time, this hauler carried a 100-ton capacity rating.

To fill in the gaps, capacity-wise, in the product line, Caterpillar introduced the "Quarry Truck" series. These were the 44-ton capacity 771C in 1992, which was replaced by the 771D in 1996, and the 65-ton 775B, also released in 1992. The 775B was upgraded into the 775D in 1995.

Caterpillar introduced its next step up in capacity with the 785 model line in late 1984, and the 789 series in 1986, which were both primarily aimed at the mining sector of the industry. Both are

strikingly similar, but the 789 is slightly larger and stands a little higher. The 785 was rated with a maximum 150-ton payload, while the 789 carried a 195-ton rating. In 1992, both trucks were upgraded to the 785B and 789B series. Today, both of these haulers are the best-selling trucks in their class-sizes, respectively, in the world.

In early 1991, Caterpillar made a bold move into the 240-ton capacity class of haulers with the introduction of the 793 series. What made this truck so newsworthy was not so much its size, but its drivetrain. At that time, all the other offerings in the 240-ton class of haulers were of a diesel-electric drive type, but the Cat entry was mechanical—that is, it utilized a transmission instead of generators

In the 195-ton capacity class of mining trucks, the Caterpillar 789B is a leader. First introduced in 1992, the Cat 789B (7EK) was the upgraded version of the original 789 (9ZC) from 1986. Power comes from a 1,705-fhp Cat 3516 EUI diesel. The powertrain is mechanical drive in nature and is completely Cat designed and built. ECO

and wheel motors. Of course, this was a highly automated and sophisticated unit with advanced electronic transmission controls. In October 1992, Caterpillar officially introduced the 793B version of the big truck with many upgrades to address the problems that had occurred during the early months of the 793 program, most notably in the transmission area. These were solved in the B series with astounding customer response. By the time this model was replaced by the 793C series in mid-1996, over 550 trucks had been sold worldwide. This was an incredible number for a hauler in the 240-ton class. The biggest notable difference in the current 793C over its predecessors is the installation of the more powerful Cat 3516B engine.

With mining companies steadily increasing the size of the shovels in their fleets, haulers with payloads exceeding 240 tons are in high demand. To meet this market need, Caterpillar has done the impossible again, by introducing a truck in the "ultra-hauler" class, as it has become known, that, like the 793 series, utilizes a mechanical drive system. It is the giant 797 hauler rated at an incredible 340–360 tons. Though the massive 1974 Terex 33-19 Titan carried a similar 350-ton payload, it did so with three axles and 10 tires. The new Cat 797 utilizes only two axles and six tires to carry its massive maximum load. To do this, the hauler was designed around 63-inch rims and wheels, utilizing the latest tire technology. Previously, the largest tire and

When Caterpillar officially released the 240-ton capacity 793 series (3SJ) of mining trucks in early 1991, it would become the world's largest mechanical-drive rear-dump hauler. All of the Cat 793's competition in the 240-ton category utilize diesel-electric drive systems. ECO

In late 1992, the original Caterpillar 793 mining truck was replaced by a new version, the Cat 793B. The 793B (1HL) used the same 2,057-fhp Cat 3516 diesel engine as the previous 793 model but now featured Electronic Unit Injection (EUI), which decreases exhaust smoke, reduces fuel consumption, and improves reliability. The capacity for both trucks remained at 240 tons. This 793B is shown shortly after delivery in 1995 at a Wyoming coal mine in the Powder River Basin. ECO

wheel combination was 57 inches. The 797 proto-type is set to be introduced into Cat's long-term field testing program in late 1998. Once again, Caterpillar is poised to prove to the mining indus-try that its advanced mechanical drive system is every bit a match—and then some—to the diesel-electric drive systems currently in use today.

Tractors and Coal Haulers

Many of Caterpillar's two-axle wheel tractors for use as either earth or coal bottom-dump haulers, were based on units derived from the scraper or rear-dump product lines. In the case of the scraper model line, the most commonly used units were the early Cater-pillar DW20 tractor with the Cat W20 bottom-dump wagon, and the 630 series tractor paired up with the Athey PW630 Bottom Dump for earth, and the Athey PH630 Bottom Dump for coal. The 660 series models were the largest of the early units. These powerful, high-speed tractors were most commonly matched up with an Athey 55-cubic yard struck capacity PW660 Bottom Dump for earth, or the 100-ton capacity PH660 Bottom Dump for coal.

In 1971, Caterpillar started to offer two high-speed tractors based on its rear-dump hauler product line. The first of these were the 768B and 772 series models. These tractors were essentially 769B and 773 haulers minus their dump boxes and hydraulics with a fifth wheel, fenders, special exhausts, and hydraulic line hookups for use by the trailers.

In 1971, Cat released the 772 Coal Hauler, rated at 100-ton capacity, and in 1975 introduced the 150-ton capacity 776 Coal Hauler. Both of these bottom-dump units were designed by Caterpillar and not supplied by an outside source. The tractors also had different serial number prefix codes as opposed to the tractors used with earth or coal bottom-dump wagons supplied by another manufacturer.

Other off-highway tractors offered by Caterpillar over the years have included the 768C in 1978; the 772B in 1978; the 776B in 1985; the 776C in 1991; the 776D in 1996; and the 784B in 1992. Only the 776D and 784B were offered in the product line in 1998.

Over the years, many allied manufacturers working with Caterpillar dealers have supplied bottom-dump wagons for use with the company's off-highway tractors. These have included Athey of Raleigh, North Carolina; Atlas of Maxter Industries Ltd. in Montreal, Quebec; WOTCO in Casper, Wyoming; and MEGA Corp. located in Albuquerque, New Mexico.

By the time the Caterpillar 793C (4AR) mining truck was released in mid-1996, over 550 units of the 793 and 793B haulers had been put into service worldwide. The improved Cat 2,166-fhp 3516B EUI engine was new to the 793C. Other new and improved features include the hydraulic systems, an enhanced transmission, and rear powertrain. Overall working empty weight of the 793C is 319,050 pounds, and 830,000 pounds with a full load. ECO

Articulated Haulers

The articulated haulers are the go-anywhere, do-anything, carry-whatever, jack-of-all-trades trucks in the earth-moving industry. Because of their four- or six-wheel-drive capabilities, and incredible maneuverability, they work in conditions that are impossible for a conventional rear dump hauler.

Caterpillar's earliest entry into the articulated hauler market actually dates back to the mid-1950s, when Cat DW15 and DW20 two-axle (four-wheel) tractors, and DW21 single-axle (two-wheel) front-end units from the scraper product line were matched to Athey rear-dump trailers, often referred to as "rockers." Just about any of Caterpillar's tractors from its scraper product lines could be hooked up to an Athey rear-dump trailer.

Today's modern articulated trucks in the Caterpillar product line can be traced directly to August 1973. That is when a new company by the name of DJB Engineering Ltd. was founded by David John Bowes Brown in Peterlee, England, for the sole purpose of building articulated trucks. From the beginning, the DJB haulers would incorporate Cat drivetrains, including engines, transmissions, and axles.

Caterpillar coal-hauling, bottom-dump haulers usually have their trailers supplied by an outside, or allied, manufacturer. In the 1960s, the 500-fhp Caterpillar 660 (90F) wheel-type tractor was matched up with a 100-ton capacity Athey PH660 coal trailer. This combination became a common sight in large coal-mining operations. This 1997 photo shows the Cat 100-ton PH660 coal hauler in an Illinois coal mine still making its daily hauling runs. Urs Peyer

These well-maintained Caterpillar 768B tractors are still at work in 1996, and pulling earth bottom-dump trailers. The 415-fhp-engined 768B (79S) was first introduced in 1971 and was in production until 1978. Urs Peyer

In 1975, Caterpillar introduced its 776 Coal Hauler, which was sold as a complete Cat unit and not as an allied joint venture with another manufacturer. The 776 Coal Hauler's tractor was a model Cat 776 (14H) that produced 870 fhp. The bottom-dump trailer (14W) was rated at 150-ton capacity. Total loaded weight of the coal hauler was 494,700 pounds. Length of the entire unit was 76 feet, 6 inches. ECO

By the autumn of 1974, the first DJB truck was unveiled—the 27.5-ton capacity D250. By June 1976, the 33-ton payload D300, which was a larger second model, was introduced. Even though these early trucks were designed by DJB, the soul of the trucks—their drivetrains—were Cat iron through and through. Many Cat dealers carried the DJB line since the drive components were fully warranteed by Caterpillar. In 1985, Caterpillar acquired the rights and designs for all of the articulated trucks from DJB Engineering, though the haulers would still be manufactured under contract in Britain. It was at this time that the DJB company name was dropped and changed to Artix Ltd. Finally, in early 1996, Caterpillar bought the manufacturing company now called Brown Group Holdings, which included

The largest tractor/bottom-dump coal haulers currently in use today, as of 1998, are the three enormous Caterpillar/MEGA CH290 units working in a North Dakota lignite coal mine. The Magnum 290-ton capacity trailer attached to the CH290 was designed by MEGA Corp. of Albuquerque, New Mexico, a long-time allied equipment manufacturer to Caterpillar. The new 789B trucks were special-ordered by the local Cat dealer and built at the Cat plant in Decatur, Illinois, with their dump bodies and hydraulic systems deleted. Final conversions, such as adding rear fenders and a fifth wheel, were performed by the dealer when the units were shipped up to North Dakota in 1995. Overall length of the CH290 is 94 feet, 8 inches and it weighs in fully loaded at a whopping 1,027,840 pounds. ECO

This specially converted new Caterpillar 777D truck was working on the Eastside Reservoir Project in southern California in 1997. The dump body and hydraulic hoists were removed, and it was turned into a tractor for towing an Atlas tandem bottom-dump train. The Atlas trailers are rated at 140- and 120-tons capacity and total 260 tons. After the truck's hauling assignment is over, the owner has the option of keeping the 777D as a tractor, or returning it to a rear dump. Urs Peyer

This recently rebuilt Caterpillar 776 tractor and Atlas RD160 heavy duty rear-dump trailer are shown working in Logan, West Virginia, in 1997. Even after many years of tough operating conditions, they perform as if they were built yesterday. Load capacity for the Atlas CH160 is a maximum 160 tons. ECO

In the Caterpillar articulated truck line, the D400E is the largest model currently offered as of 1998. First introduced as the replacement for the D400D in 1995, the D400E (2YR) is powered by a 385-fhp Cat 3406 diesel engine. Load capacity for the hauler is 40 tons. With 6x6 all-wheel drive and limited slip differentials on all axles, the D400E is designed for maximum performance in the toughest working conditions imaginable. Caterpillar, Inc.

all of the facilities and property in Peterlee, England. This made everything involved with the production and building of articulated trucks 100-percent Caterpillar. Also, an additional factory being built in Waco, Texas, will supply articulated haulers for the North American and Latin American markets at the turn of the century.

There have been numerous models and variations of these articulated haulers built over the years. These include two-axle, four-wheel-drive models;

three-axle, four-wheel-drive models; and three-axle, six-wheel-drive versions. The largest two-axle models built were the DJB/Caterpillar D44, from 1981 to 1986, and the Cat D44B, from 1986 to 1987. Both were rated with 44-ton payloads. The largest three-axle units were the DJB/Caterpillar D550, from 1978 to 1986, and the short-lived Cat D550B, from 1986 to 1987. These trucks carried 55-ton payloads, more than any other articulated built at that time.

CHAPTER 7

The Hydraulic Excavators

As Caterpillar entered the 1970s, the company was lagging behind in the hydraulic excavator field and sales in the marketplace were growing at an ever-increasing rate. Many U.S. companies were well ahead of Cat in the development and production of these machines, some of which included Warner & Swasey, Bucyrus-Erie, Link-Belt, and Koehring. Many of these companies already produced cable-type backhoe excavators, which also gave them a further advantage, with years of in-the-field experience concerning these types of machines. Hydraulic excavators were also well established in the Western European market by various overseas companies. But Cat was not

The first Caterpillar 245 (95V) model series was originally introduced in 1974, with a power rating of 325 fhp and an average bucket capacity of 3 cubic yards. The Cat 245B Series II (6MF) was released in 1990 with more power and larger buckets. The 245B II was rated at 360 fhp with a 5- to 6.75-cubic yard backhoe capacity range. Overall working weight of the standard excavator was 143,520 pounds. Urs Peyer

Introduced in 1972, the Caterpillar 225 excavator was the first hydraulic model 100-percent designed and built by the company. With 125 fhp and an average 1-cubic yard bucket, the Cat 225 (51U) was not the largest machine on the block by any means. But it would set the pace for larger and more sophisticated excavators yet to come from the company. Urs Peyer

The popular Caterpillar 350L (2ZL) excavator was first released in 1993. The 350L carries a power rating of 286 fhp and is classified as a 1.38- to 3.50-cubic yard machine. The version pictured is equipped with an optional demolition grapple attachment instead of the standard bucket. Any number of outside manufacturers produce this type of equipment for use on most of Caterpillar's various excavator models. Caterpillar produces its own specialized demolition attachments under the Balderson name and recently expanded its offerings with the purchase in 1996 of Vibra-Ram, a German producer of such attachments. Urs Peyer

just going to sit on the sidelines and let this promising market for hydraulic machines pass by. In 1972, the company was ready to start writing its own history on hydraulic excavators, starting with the release of the newly designed Cat 225 series.

The Caterpillar 225 was a smart-looking machine powered by a single Cat 3160 eight-cylinder diesel engine rated at 125 fhp. Later versions would receive the improved 3208 powerplant. Propulsion was by twin hydrostatic drive

hydraulic motors on the tracks. The model 225 was 100-percent Cat designed and built.

In 1973, the second model in the Cat hydraulic excavator product line was introduced—the 235. Slightly larger than the 225, the 235 was powered by a Cat 3306 six-cylinder diesel engine rated at 195 fhp.

The third new model produced by Cat was released as the model 245 in 1974. The Cat 245 was considerably larger than the 235 series. Not only

The largest of the 300 Series models of Caterpillar excavators is Cat's 375 LME Mass Excavator. Released in 1993, the 375 LME (1JM) is powered by a 428-fhp Cat 3406C diesel engine. The capacity range for the ME version is 4.75 to 5.75 cubic yards. Maximum overall working weight is 180,366 pounds. ECO

was it a very powerful-looking machine, it was a powerful performing machine as well, equipped with a Cat 3406 diesel engine rated at 325 fhp. Average operating weight of the 245 was 143,520 pounds, as compared to the weight of the model 235 at 86,700 pounds.

The Cat 225, 235, and 245, along with the smaller model 215 from 1976, served front-line duty for the company in the battle for excavator market share. But as Caterpillar found itself coming out of the troubled recessionary times of the early 1980s, many of its former competitors were gone, unable to weather the changing worldwide marketplace. Japanese companies such as Komatsu and Hitachi had taken their place. These firms' technical expertise in the manufacturing of construction equipment, especially hydraulic excavators, was taking the North American market by

After the Caterpillar 235 (32K) excavator was released in 1973, an additional front shovel model, the 235 FS (81X), was introduced in 1978. This model was rated at 195 fhp and was offered with two bucket choices: a 3-cubic yard front dump, or a 2.38-cubic yard bottom dump. This model was replaced by the 235B FS (1FD) in 1986. Pictured working in 1993 is a Belgium-built Cat 235 FS (83X). The model built in Belgium was first introduced in 1979. Urs Peyer

storm. If Caterpillar was going to compete globally in this market segment, it needed allies.

Starting in 1984, Cat introduced new model lines of smaller excavators, manufactured by Eder of Germany, a well-respected name in the production of hydraulic machines in Europe. Tracked machines included the models 205, 211, and 213. Excavators mounted on wheeled chassis were the models 206, 212, 214, and 224. These models filled in the gaps in the product line in sizes smaller than the Cat 215 series.

But Cat had an ace up its sleeve. Back in 1962, Caterpillar had announced that it was forming an equal-ownership manufacturing and marketing company with Mitsubishi, to be called Caterpillar Mitsubishi Ltd. This was done to get around stringent Japanese import controls. Cat products to be built in Japan would include tracked dozers and loaders, and wheel loaders. The venture was fully implemented in 1963 with the first product, a D4 tractor, produced in the spring of 1965. The partnership was very successful for both companies,

The front-shovel version of the Caterpillar 245 excavator was first released in 1977. The Cat 245 FS (82X) was powered by a Cat 3406 diesel engine rated at 325 fhp. Bucket choices were a 5-cubic yard front dump and a 4-cubic yard bottom dump. Overall working weight was 147,575 pounds. Urs Peyer

and in 1987 the joint venture was expanded to include hydraulic excavators. The new venture was renamed Shin Caterpillar Mitsubishi Ltd.

Caterpillar's global strategy was starting to fall into place in regards to its excavator product line. The company's venture in Japan made way for a flood of new models in 1987. Some of these were the E110, E120, E140, E200B, E240, E300, E450, and E650 series of hydraulic excavators.

Today, Cat's 300 Series excavators are some of the finest machines available anywhere in the world. Some of the latest offerings include the impressive 345B L, the versatile 350, and the largest in the series, the 375. The model 375 replaced the older, but highly respected 245D model in 1993. New models introduced in 1999 include the 340 and 360 series of machines.

Some of Caterpillar's early excavators were also offered as hydraulic front shovels. This model variation was available on the 235, 235B, 235C, 245, 245B, 245D, E450, and E650 series of excavators.

For larger quarry and mining operations

This new Caterpillar 245B FS, pictured in 1990, is a fairly rare machine since few front-shovel versions of this model were built. The U.S. (6MF) and Belgium (1SJ) built shovels were powered by a 360-fhp Cat 3406B diesel. Bucket capacities were the same as in the previous 245 FS model. Working weight of the bottom-dump-bucket equipped shovel was 152,440 pounds. Urs Peyer

The smallest of the 5000 Series mining excavators is the Caterpillar 5080 front shovel, which was introduced in 1993. The Cat 5080 (8SL) shares many of its components with its backhoe alter ego—the 375L excavator. The 5080 is powered by a Cat 3406C diesel engine churning out 428 fhp. Bucket capacity is 6.8 cubic yards with an average operating weight of 184,800 pounds. ECO

where large and powerful front shovels and mass excavators (ME) are required, Caterpillar offers its 5000 Series of hydraulic machines. The first model in this product line to be introduced was the Cat 5130 Front Shovel, first publicly shown at the October 1992 MINExpo in Las Vegas, Nevada, and officially released in late 1993. The size of the 5130 series put it in direct competition with some well-established products in the mining excavator field from such manufacturers as O&K, Demag, Liebherr from Germany, and Hitachi from Japan. The model 5130 was built entirely by Caterpillar in

North America, and primarily designed to load haul trucks in the 60- to 100-ton capacity class. In mid-1997, Cat introduced the improved "B" version of the 5130. The new 5130B carried more weight, produced more power, and carried a larger bucket compared to its predecessor.

The smallest excavator presently in the 5000 Series is the Cat 5080 Front Shovel. Introduced in late 1993, the 5080 is based heavily on the 375 series. In most respects, the 5080 is the front-shovel version of the 375 ME. Originally only built at Cat's manufacturing facilities in Belgium,

Introduced in October 1992, the Caterpillar 5130 (7TJ) front shovel was the first of the 5000 Series mining excavators to be announced. The 5130 was powered by a Cat 755-fhp 3508 diesel engine with a front-shovel capacity ranging from 11 to 13.75 cubic yards. Not long after the front-shovel model went into full production in late 1993, a backhoe ME (Mass Excavator) version was released. The power ratings were the same as in the shovel version; bucket capacities ranged from 10.2 to 17.8 cubic yards, and it had a maximum 27-feet, 6-inch digging depth. Working weight of the backhoe 5130 ME was 390,000 pounds. ECO

By July 1997, an improved Caterpillar 5130B model replaced the previous 5130 version. An 800-fhp Cat 3508B provided the new model's power. Capacity for the B version shovel was now up to 14.5 cubic yards, and the ME version's range was rated at 10.5 to 24 cubic yards. Working weight for the shovel is 399,000 pounds and 401,000 pounds for the backhoe ME version. ECO

production was also started on the 5080 in the United States in 1995. The unit is also available as the 5080 MH (Material Handler), specially suited for scrap metal handling.

The largest hydraulic excavator currently built by Caterpillar is its model 5230. Field testing of the prototype unit, at a Utah phosphate mine, took place throughout most of 1993 with the production version officially announced by mid-1994. The Cat 5230 is built in the United States and contains some of the largest castings ever to come out of the company's foundries. The 5230 is

The largest excavator currently built by Caterpillar is the model 5230. The Cat 5230 (7LL) was first introduced into field testing in 1993 with the production version officially released in mid-1994. A 1470-fhp Cat 3516 sixteen-cylinder engine provides the 5230's motivation. Maximum bucket capacity for the front-shovel version is 22.2 cubic yards with an overall working weight of 693,800 pounds. This 5230 shovel is shown working at a coal mine in eastern Kentucky in 1995. ECO

After the release of the 5230 front shovel, a backhoe ME version soon followed. The 5230 ME bucket capacity range is from 20.3 to 31.2 cubic yards with a total machine weight of 692,320 pounds. The power ratings are the same in both versions of the excavator. The 5230 ME shown here at work in a coal mine in western Pennsylvania in 1997 has a maximum reach of 58 feet. Its 20.3-cubic yard bucket can load the mine's 150-ton capacity haulers in four quick passes. ECO

a massive machine, weighing in at 693,800 pounds for the front shovel (FS) and 692,320 pounds for the backhoe (ME) version. The big excavator is powered by a single Cat 3516 sixteen-cylinder diesel engine, rated at 1,575 gross horsepower and 1,470 fhp. The 5230 FS has a maximum bucket size of 22.2 cubic yards, while the ME version is rated at 20.3 cubic yards for the standard bucket and 31.2 cubic yards for a coal-loading version. The 5230 was designed mainly for use in the mining industry, specifically sized to load 150- to 200-ton capacity haul trucks.

CHAPTER 8

Modern Agricultural Machines

Over the last few decades, Caterpillar has been a recognized leader in the construction and mining equipment industry. But in the last few years, the company has been a trendsetter in the agricultural tractor market as well. Caterpillar has *always* manufactured crawler-tractors for its agricultural farming customers who work where low compaction of the soil or difficult field conditions exist. After all, the company's earliest ancestors, Best and Holt, were the first to create and sell their machinery to the farming market, which sent the horse and mule teams back to the barn to stay.

The advantages of crawler-type tractors over rubber-tired models, in certain working conditions, are less soil compaction due to the lower ground

The in-line six-cylinder Cat 3196 ATAAC diesel engine rated at 370 gross horsepower and 310 PTO horsepower, made the Caterpillar Challenger 85D series a top-performing agricultural tractor. The chassis and overall size of the Challenger 85D was the same as the 75D and 65D models—only the engines and power ratings were different. ECO

In 1997, Caterpillar started offering its Challenger models 35, 45, and 55 with an adjustable wide-track "Mobil-trac" system. With adjustable track widths ranging from 80 to 120 inches, these tractors are ideally suited for row crop field applications. The wide-track Challenger 45 pictured here is shown pulling a Cat VFS70 (Versatile Floatation System) "Mobil-trac" high-flotation crawler and frame attachment. This platform system allows a wide variety of hauling and spreading equipment to be attached to them, such as this Orthman grain transporter. ECO

pressure exerted by a continuous track, greater overall traction, better stability when working on slopes, and high usable drawbar power. In the past, Cat machines always had the drawbar power. The problem was with the transmissions or, more accurately, the selected gear and speed ratios. This was solved in 1966 with the introduction of the first Caterpillar Special Application Tractor, the D4D SA. The Cat machines offered special transmissions with closely spaced speeds, enabling the operator to match work requirements in the key 2.5- to 5-mile-per-hour tillage range. Other popular tractors introduced in this series were the D5 SA in 1967;

the D6C SA in 1970; the D7G SA in 1977; and, for the really tough jobs, the D8L SA in 1984.

The crawler farm tractors had some built-in disadvantages because of their metal tracks. Overall speed was much slower than rubber-tired tractors, thus, less mobility, and these machines could not be

Right: *Starting in 1997, German agricultural equipment manufacturer Claas, and Caterpillar, Inc. agreed to a marketing arrangement in which Cat Challenger tractors could be sold and serviced in Europe through the Claas dealer network. Even though they are painted the Claas colors of green and white, they are still Cat Challengers through and through.* Urs Peyer

This view of the wide-track Cat Challenger 45 certainly emphasizes the large-diameter rear-drive wheel that helps provide additional crop clearance when working in 30-inch rows. As with the larger Challengers, the models 35, 45, and 55 all share the same chassis. Only the engines are different. ECO

The most powerful "Mobil-trac" agricultural tractor to be released by Caterpillar, as of 1998, is the Challenger 95E. Introduced in the autumn of 1997, the 95E is powered by a Cat 3196C engine cranking out 410 gross horsepower and 353 PTO horsepower. The Challenger 95E also shares its new bodywork with the 85E, 75E, and 65E tractors, which were also released at the same time. The "Special Application Drive Wheel" on this 95E features tapered drive slots between drive elements. This allows mud and debris to extrude through the wheel, eliminating belt-to-driver slippage in most sloppy and muddy field conditions. Caterpillar, Inc.

driven on public roads without causing damage to the surface. The solution was simple to Cat engineers. Why not make the tracks in the form of a continuous rubber belt, instead of metal links? And that is just what the company set out to do. Starting in 1982, Caterpillar returned to the farming valleys of California that had been so important during the development of its crawler-tractor. Prototypes of modified crawler models with a revolutionary rubber track system were put to the test. At first the early experimental machines were based on Cat D6D models, but other modified units, such as the D3B and D4E, soon joined the testing program.

In 1987, after five years and thousands of hours

of testing, the new tractor was finally officially released as the Caterpillar Challenger 65. Sleek and very modern looking, it was unlike any crawler the company had ever produced. The Challenger 65 was equipped with the newly designed "Mobil-trac System." Mobil-trac transferred the tractor's power to the ground through one-piece rubber belts, reinforced with continuous flexible steel cables bonded into the rubber compound. These belts provided a large ground contact area, lowering soil compaction in the fields, and also allowed the tractor to be driven on roads without damaging the paved surfaces. The Challenger 65 was powered by a Cat 3306 DITA diesel engine, rated at 270 gross horsepower and 256 fhp, with 235 PTO horsepower available.

Over the years, various models of the original Challenger 65 concept have been released with many mechanical improvements. These have included the Challenger 65B in late 1990; the 65C in late 1992; and the 65D in late 1994. Other Cat Challenger model types that have also found similar success have been the 70C in 1993; the 75 in late 1990; the 75C in late 1992; the 75D in 1996; the 85C in 1993; and the 85D in 1996. In late 1997, the entire large Challenger tractor lineup was upgraded into the new E series. New models included the 65E, 75E, 85E, and the even more-powerful 95E. Along with the usual component improvements, the E series Challengers also sported new bodywork with a more rounded design and a very striking appearance.

Cat followed the success of the larger Challenger series in 1994 with the addition of a new line of Challengers specially designed for row crop farming. The first of the row crop Challengers released, the Models 35 and 45, were equipped with a more radical form of the Cat Mobil-trac System than that found on the larger models. The row crop tractors feature large-diameter rear-drive wheels for late season cultivation. This gives the Challengers a kind of "hot rod" appearance at first glance. In 1995, Cat added another model to the row crop tractor lineup identified as the Challenger 55. This tractor makes use of the more powerful Cat 3126 diesel engine, with a drawbar rating of 191 horsepower and a PTO rating of 225 horsepower. These models all share the same ultra sleek bodywork that served as a design guide for the larger E series models.

The Cat Challenger "ag" machines played a dominant role in the rubber-tracked farm tractor field. But in late 1997, John Deere, the world's leader in farm machinery, introduced its own design of a prototype rubber-tracked machine, looking much like the Challenger's. This John Deere has a track pitch that is more pronounced than the larger Cat machines, but not as radical as the row crop units. Cat could not keep such a good thing all to itself forever.

Caterpillar moved into uncharted waters again in late 1997 with the introduction of four new models of combines, named the LEXION 460, 465, 480, and 485. The new combine product line is a joint venture between Caterpillar and Claas of Germany, a very popular name in the European agricultural manufacturing sector. The Cat LEXION is based on the Claas-designed combines, and are offered in two harvesting separation family groups. The 460/465 units feature six straw walkers to increase the amount of agitation, which helps capture more grain. The 480/485 uses a rotary separation system for high-capacity harvesting in the toughest conditions. The LEXION 460 and 480 feature conventional tires and wheels at all four corners. The 465 and 485 offer Cat's innovative rubber Mobil-trac system on the front axle, allowing the combines to harvest in soft field conditions. Contemporary in look and in design, the Cat LEXIONs have John Deere and Case set firmly in their sights.

Introduced in late 1997, the Caterpillar LEXION 485 combine harvester is another product line benefit of the Cat and Claas marketing agreement. The German-designed LEXION 485 featured here is powered by a Cat 3176 diesel engine rated at 365 horsepower. Also included on this LEXION 485 is a rotary separation system, a 12-row corn header, and the Cat "Mobil-trac" undercarriage in the front. ECO

CHAPTER 9

Into the Next Century

Even though the Caterpillar name is synonymous with dozers and other "classic" earthmoving machines, these are only part of the company's past and future in the global heavy equipment marketplace. This is why the name of the Caterpillar Tractor Company was changed in 1986 to Caterpillar, Inc., to better reflect all of its divisions as a whole corporate structure.

Additional Caterpillar product lines include forestry skidders and log loaders, telescopic handlers, integrated toolcarriers, cold planers, asphalt pavers, road reclaimers and stabilizers, vibratory- and pneumatic-tired compactors, pipelayers, diesel

Introduced in 1993, the Tiger 690D wheel dozer was a replacement for the previous 690B model that had been in service since 1985. The 690D was based heavily on the Caterpillar 992D wheel loader. The front blade hydraulic system was also incorporated from the Cat D10N dozer. The engine in the 690D was the proven 690-fhp Cat 3412 diesel. The 690D, shown working in a North Dakota coal mine in 1995, was one of the first Tigers equipped with a rear-mounted ripper. ECO

and gas turbine engines, and underground mining machines. Many of these equipment offerings evolved from the more established product lineups, while others were added through the buyouts of other manufacturers, acquisitions of technology, or joint ventures where Caterpillar has formed a partnership with another company in building and marketing a shared product concern.

In 1984, Caterpillar and CMI Corporation of Oklahoma formed a manufacturing and marketing agreement for the production of paving prod-ucts. In 1987, the association between the two companies was discontinued. But Caterpillar was able to purchase from CMI the technology to manufacture pavement profilers, asphalt pavers, soil stabilizers, and road reclaimers. They were also able to buy CMI's wholly-owned subsidiary, RayGo, Inc. of Minnesota, which added a broad range of soil and asphalt compactors. Cat increased its paving-product offerings in April 1991, when the company purchased Barber-Greene, a world-renowned producer of paving

Introduced at the September 1996 MINExpo in Las Vegas as the replacement for the 690D, was the Tiger 790G. Based on the new 992G wheel loader, the 790G is a big and powerful machine and is in fact the world's largest production wheel dozer. Using the same drivetrain found in the 992G, the power is rated at 800 fhp. A 20-foot, 8-inch semi-U, or a 23-foot, 8-inch coal blade are the two types offered. Average operating weight is 218,756 pounds. After Caterpillar bought the complete manufacturing rights to the 790G from Tiger Engineering Pty, Ltd. in the autumn of 1997, the wheel dozer was redesignated the Cat 854G in 1998. ECO

The Elphinstone underground rear-dump haulers are based on Caterpillar truck designs. This 55-ton capacity Elphinstone 73B is a modified Cat 773 series hauler, specially equipped for low clearance and restrictive underground mine working environments. In 1997, the 73B was replaced by the newer 58-ton capacity 73D version, which is based on the Cat 773D. Caterpillar, Inc.

machines. All of these products are marketed through Caterpillar Paving Products, Inc.

As Caterpillar enters the twenty-first century, it does so with the broadest and strongest product lines ever offered in the company's history. New products are constantly created, and new equipment is added. In the autumn of 1997, Caterpillar purchased the rights to the large wheel dozers produced by Tiger Engineering Pty, Ltd. of Australia. Tiger has been producing large rubber-tired wheel dozers since introducing its first model, the 690A, in late 1981. Tiger dozers complement and suitably blend into the Caterpillar lineup because they are based largely on Cat components, and have always been sold and serviced through the Cat dealer network. Other past Tiger models have include the 690B, which was based on the Cat 992C, and the 690D, based on the Cat 992D. The current models purchased by Caterpillar include the Tiger 590B, introduced in the spring of 1994 and based on the Cat 990 wheel loader, and the Tiger 790G, first announced in September 1996. The Tiger 790G is based on the new Cat 992G wheel loader. Both units were integrated into the Caterpillar wheel dozer product line in 1998, with new model designations that correspond with previous Cat wheel dozer nomenclature. The Tiger 590B became the Cat 844, and the Tiger 790G is now referred to as the Cat 854G.

Caterpillar also has Australian ties in the underground mining equipment industry. Caterpillar Elphinstone Pty, Ltd. is the joint-venture company of Caterpillar, Inc. and Dale B. Elphinstone Pty, Ltd. located in Tasmania, Australia. Elphinstone manufactures underground mining equipment, which includes Load-Haul-Dump (LHD) loaders, and rigid-frame and articulated haulers. All "Elphies" utilize Cat drivetrains, with

the rigid frame trucks based heavily on regular-production Cat haulers such as the 769D and 773D. The designs of the low-profile LHD loaders and the articulated haulers are Elphinstone designs, but contain various Cat components, including the engines and transmissions.

Some of Caterpillar's newest product lines were introduced in 1998, which include mini-hydraulic excavators and skid-steer loaders. Many of these machines will be powered by Perkins engines, which Caterpillar purchased in December 1997 from Lucas Varity Plc. of England. This assures Caterpillar complete product control of its machines in the expanding sales market of compact construction equipment.

In the world of heavy equipment, Caterpillar is without equal when it comes to equipment choices, production, dealerships, technological innovations, and manpower. It is no wonder that the town of Peoria, Illinois, the home of Caterpillar's corporate offices, is known as the "earth-moving capital of the world."

No matter what the size of the project, from the smallest driveway paving assignment to the largest copper mining operation, rest assured that Caterpillar "iron" will be on the job—as they have been in the past, and as they will continue to be in the future.

INDEX